THE MEZZE COOKBOOK

SHARING PLATES FROM THE MIDDLE EAST

THE MEZZE COOKBOOK
SHARING PLATES FROM THE MIDDLE EAST

Salma Hage

Introduction
6

CHAPTER ONE
Basics
8

CHAPTER TWO
Dips & Nibbles
30

CHAPTER THREE
Salads
64

CHAPTER FOUR
Vegetables
86

CHAPTER FIVE
Stuffed & Fried
124

CHAPTER SIX
Grains, Pulses & Rice
150

CHAPTER SEVEN
Pastries & Breads
186

CHAPTER EIGHT
Sweets
218

CHAPTER NINE
Drinks
250

Glossary & Index
264

An introduction to a mezze way of eating

When I arrived in London from Lebanon in the 1960s, the idea of everyone sitting around the table with solo plates of meat and a boiled vegetable or two, all seemed very strange to me. Though I have come to love English food in the years since, I have always craved the sociable food from my homeland: flatbreads to tear, topped with za'atar and grassy olive oil; fresh, vibrant tabbouleh with everyone diving in for a third or fourth helping; and my very favorite—stuffed phyllo (filo) rolls, the perfect finger food to pick over whilst sharing stories with friends and family.

Depending on who you ask, mezze is a selection of smaller-sized seasonal dishes to share, either before a main meal, or as the main meal itself. "Proper" mezze, is usually found in restaurants, or at celebrations or parties in the Middle East, since it is often considered a lot of dishes for a someone to make in one go at home. Though of course it will depend on where you are, a general guide would be to expect the cold dishes to come first—salads, bright pickles, olives, white cheese in olive oil, labneh, hummus, babaganoush, always several types of bread. Then the warm platters would begin, maybe little kibbeh, stuffed with lamb or vegetables, warmed grain salads, freekeh, piping-hot falafel, some meat or fish, ful medames. The meal could go on for hours, and easily amount to twenty-something plates. It might finally be rounded off with a few more olives, some seasonal fruits and lots of strong, bitter Arabic coffee.

Though we seldom ate at restaurants, because we simply couldn't afford to when I was a child, many of these little dishes were all familiar to me as I had grown up eating variants of them at home in Lebanon, though rarely all at once.

My mother was only fourteen when she had me, so my grandmother cared for me a lot and she was a brilliant cook. She would char eggplants (aubergines) directly over the fire, letting them collapse into a smoky heap that tasted delicious mixed with garlic and bread. We would make m'juderah—a humble lentil dish with onions—which was the very first thing I remember making by myself, and we'd often pick dandelions together, boiling them and serving with lemon juice, garlic and plenty of bread. Another favorite was fasolia, which I would help prepare when I was very young.

As I got older and married in Lebanon, whenever I cooked a dish, I would save a helping or two for my neighbor, and she always did the same. We would swap dishes and have a chat, making lunch so much more enjoyable. If a guest turned up unexpectedly at my house, even now in London, they would always be offered something to eat, whatever the time. If my family is eating, we will gladly lay an extra place, or if not, even if it is midnight, there will be a homemade pastry or falafel to warm them up. We will eat even the simplest meal (which is often a mix of Lebanese and English in my house now) together, dipping in and out of each other's plates with plenty of bread or salad leaves, passing everything between us. When I go back to Lebanon, I sometimes forget it is considered rude to clean your plate as it shows that you are still hungry enough to eat more!

For me, all of these social customs sum up Middle Eastern cuisine in so many ways. Mezze is a mixture of all of these traditions—sharing food, celebrating being together, having plenty on the table, and welcoming new faces.

In today's modern world, whether in the East or the West, making lots of smaller dishes to share is a brilliant way of eating. Many of the dishes can be prepared in advance, and they can easily be mixed and matched to make a meal that suits you. People with different diets, be they gluten free or vegetarian—as many of my family are—can all be accommodated. The recipes in this book are designed to be small plates made from a healthy variety of ingredients. Some of them are more traditional dishes that I grew up with, and some are newer ideas that I have tried and tested in my home in London.

We don't have much of a tradition really of eating dessert at the end of a meal, you'd be more likely to be offered a date or some fresh fruit in Lebanon. The sweets are usually saved to have with coffee mid morning or afternoon, but I think they're too good to keep for the daylight hours, so I've included lots of ideas to finish off your savory mezze spreads with too. Blood orange Turkish delight is a delicious way to round off a rich meal, or try the baked quinces for a sticky grown-up treat.

By all means, prepare a full mezze feast for your loved ones, and keep the dishes coming like there is no tomorrow, or make a smaller selection and eat them at the beginning of a meal—some home marinated olives and a falafel make an excellent starter. I have suggested some menu ideas on the next page. Otherwise, they work very well as larger dishes on their own. However you use my recipes, I hope you enjoy making them.

Menu Ideas

PICNIC
Mograbieh (Giant Couscous) Salad (p.71)
Cabbage and Apple Slaw (p.117)
Zucchini Kuku (p.120)
Homemade Spicy Lamb Sausage (p.138)
Kale and Chile Rolls (p.208)
Spinach and Walnut Tartlets (p.210)
Favorite Ma'mool Cookies (p.222)
Tahini Brownies (p.223)
Hibiscus and Mint Iced Tea (p.260)

CLASSIC
Babaganoush (p.32)
Classic Falafel (p.44)
Preserved Lemon and Bay-Scented Olives (p.49)
Hummus with Lamb and Pine Nuts (p.58)
Winter Tabbouleh (p.70)
Fasolia (p.158)
Ful Medames (p.175)
Lentil and Bulgar Wheat M'juderah (p.178)
Large Lamb Kibbeh (p.184)
Pecan and Orange Baklava (p.242)
Blood Orange and Pistachio Turkish Delight (p.246)
Rose and Cinnamon Tea (p.257)

MODERN
Tahini and Grape Molasses Dip (p.33)
Tahini Rémoulade (p.78)
Labneh with Figs and Candied Walnuts (p.80)
Cauliflower Couscous with Pine Nuts and Raisins (p.82)
Shredded Brussels Sprouts with Walnuts (p.92)
Za'atar Mushrooms with Buckwheat Pancakes (p.94)
Fried Potatoes with Fennel and Green Olives (p.111)
Harissa Sweet Potato Cakes (p.128)
Fava Bean and Artichoke Tartlets (p.206)
Rose and Cardamon Shortbread (p.243)
Beet Juice (p.252)
Raspberry Rose Lemonade (p.262)

DINNER
Roasted Baby Beets with Za'atar Labneh (p.38)
Charred Cauliflower with Pickled Apple (p.66)
Green Bean and Hazelnut Salad (p.68)
Grilled Purple Sprouting Broccoli and Halloumi (p.116)
Carrot and Pistachio Fritters (p.131)
Wild Rice Salad with Roasted Root Vegetables (p.164)
Whole Baked Squash with Quinoa (p.170)
Smoky Eggplant and Cilantro Tartlets (p.207)
Fish Shawarma (p.216)
Baked Cardamom and Almond Milk Rice Pudding (p.228)
Arabic Coffee Mousse (p.234)

CHAPTER ONE
Basics

Labneh (Strained Yogurt Cheese)

PREPARATION TIME
5 minutes + 6 hours standing time

COOKING TIME
—

MAKES
about 9 oz (250 g)

2 cups (1 lb/450 g) thick Greek yogurt
pinch of salt, or to taste
3 tablespoons extra virgin olive oil
Za'atar (see page 13), for sprinkling (optional)

Yogurt, strained to remove the whey, is wonderfully thick and indulgent. I like labneh simply drizzled with olive oil and sprinkled with za'atar but it makes a perfect base for salads and a quick filling for sandwiches too.

You can also make this using plain rather than Greek yogurt; if so, allow it to stand in the cheesecloth (muslin) for an extra 3 hours.

PREPARATION

Line a strainer (sieve) with a double thickness of cheesecloth (muslin) and set over a large bowl. Pour in the yogurt, cover with the sides of the cheesecloth. Place in the refrigerator for at least 6 hours until thickened and all the liquid has drained off.

Check occasionally to make sure the bottom of the strainer is not touching the liquid. If it is, pour away the liquid.

Season the labneh with salt to taste, then spread out on a plate. Drizzle with olive oil and dust with za'atar, if wished. Best chilled before serving.

Lebanese 7-Spice Seasoning

PREPARATION TIME
5 minutes

COOKING TIME
—

MAKES
1 ¾ cups (6 oz/175 g)

- 5 tablespoons ground allspice
- 3 ½ tablespoons ground black pepper
- 3 ½ tablespoons ground cinnamon
- 5 tablespoons ground cloves
- 4 tablespoons grated nutmeg
- 4 tablespoons ground fenugreek
- 4 tablespoons ground ginger

See pages 14–15 for image

This is my version of a classic Lebanese spice blend, although many families will have their own take on it. For me, it encapsulates the flavor of Lebanese cooking. Just a teaspoon of this transforms so many dishes. Like all ground spice blends, though, it won't keep forever; stored in an airtight jar, it should last for up to 6 months.

PREPARATION
Mix all the ingredients together and store in an airtight container for up to 6 months.

Tahini

PREPARATION TIME
10 minutes

COOKING TIME
—

MAKES
1 (12-oz/350-ml) jar

- 2 cups (9 oz/250 g) toasted sesame seeds
- 1 teaspoon sea salt
- ½–⅔ cup (4–5 fl oz/120–150ml) olive oil, depending on taste

See pages 14–15 for image

Tahini, as common in the Middle East as peanut butter is in the West, is now readily available in most supermarkets. The store-bought variety is less flavorsome than the homemade though, so it's worth the extra effort.

PREPARATION
Put the seeds and salt into a food processor or high-speed blender with half of the oil and process. Use a spatula to scrape down the sides and add the rest of the oil gradually, adding more to taste, if necessary.

Pour into a sterilized jar (see page 26) with a screw-top lid. Store in the refrigerator for up to a month. If the tahini separates, stir to combine.

Za'atar

PREPARATION TIME	COOKING TIME	MAKES
5 minutes	10 minutes	scant 1 cup (6 oz/175 g)

7 tablespoons fresh thyme, stems removed
2 tablespoons dried thyme
1 teaspoon dried marjoram
2 teaspoons sumac
3 tablespoons sesame seeds, toasted
sea salt, to taste

See pages 14–15 for image

Za'atar is a herb that grows along the Syrian/Lebanese border. In English it is sometimes known as wild thyme. In cooking, though, za'atar more commonly refers to this aromatic herb and seed blend. Use it on everything from bread drizzled with olive oil to labneh (see page 10).

PREPARATION

Preheat the oven to 300°F/150°C/Gas Mark 2.

Spread the fresh thyme leaves on a baking sheet and dry in the oven for about 10 minutes, or until the leaves crumble easily. Let cool.

Crumble the thyme with your fingers. Add to a mortar with the dried thyme, marjoram, sumac, and sea salt and crush with the pestle. Once an even consistency is achieved, add the toasted sesame seeds and stir before using. Store in an airtight container for up to 6 months.

1. Pink Pickled Turnips (p.16) 2. Lebanese 7-Spice Seasoning (p.12) 3. Spiced Pickled Carrots (p.17) 4. Tahini (p.12) 5. Za'atar (p.13)

Pink Pickled Turnips

PREPARATION TIME	COOKING TIME	MAKES
20 minutes + 10 minutes cooling + 1 week standing time	5 minutes	1 (50-fl oz/1.5-liter) jar

1 lb 2 oz/500 g turnips, peeled and cut into ¼-inch/5-mm rounds
1 small beet (beetroot), peeled and cut into ¼-inch/5-mm rounds
1 bay leaf
1 garlic clove, finely sliced
3 heaping tablespoons (1 ½ oz/ 40 g) golden superfine (caster) sugar
3 scant tablespoons (1 ½ oz/ 40 g) salt
1 cup (8 fl oz/250 ml) white wine vinegar

See pages 14–15 for image

In this recipe, turnips are stained bright pink naturally with beets. They are the perfect accompaniment to falafel, or to add heat and interest to a mezze spread. They are incredibly easy to make and just need a week of resting time before they're ready to eat. Use a transparent glass jar—they're so pretty to look at.

PREPARATION
Lay the turnip and beet (beetroot) rounds flat on a chopping board, stacking 2 or 3 similar-size ones on top of one another, then slice into thin matchsticks. Set the chopped vegetables aside in a large bowl.

Put the bay leaf, garlic, sugar, and salt in a medium saucepan, and cover with the vinegar and generous 2 cups (17 fl oz/500ml) water. Heat gently until the sugar and salt have dissolved (you do not need to let it boil). Let cool for 10 minutes.

Pack the chopped vegetables into a large sterilized 50-fl oz (1.5-liter) jar (see page 26) and cover with the cooled pickling liquid, leaving a 1-inch (2-cm) head space.

Allow the jar to stand uncovered, until the liquid cools completely, then cover the jar with the lid and store in a cool, dark place for up to 3 months. Wait a week before eating, during which time the turnips will turn bright pink from the beets. They are good with the Classic Falafel (see page 44) or alongside some Classic Hummus (see page 45) and pita bread.

Spiced Pickled Carrots

PREPARATION TIME	COOKING TIME	MAKES
10 minutes + 10 minutes cooling + 1 week standing time	10 minutes	3 or 4 (10-fl oz/300-ml) jars

1 tablespoon cumin seeds
1 tablespoon black peppercorns
seeds of 12 cardamom pods
1 tablespoon coriander seeds
2 bay leaves
4 garlic cloves, peeled
1 ½ cups (12 fl oz/350 ml) white wine vinegar
2 tablespoons coarse sea salt
2 tablespoons golden superfine (caster) sugar
2 ¼ lb/1 kg carrots, peeled and cut into ½-inch/1-cm rounds or thin matchsticks (or a mixture)

See pages 14–15 for image

I use some of my favorite spices to add interest to these carrots, but I'm sure the addition of some caraway seeds in place of the cumin, or a whole chile to add a bit of heat, would work well too.

PREPARATION
Toast the cumin seeds, peppercorns, cardamom seeds, and coriander seeds in a medium saucepan for 1 minute over a medium heat, until they smell fragrant (but are not browning). Add the bay leaves, garlic, vinegar, salt, and sugar to the pan, along with 1 ½ cups (12 fl oz/350 ml) water. Bring to a gentle simmer to dissolve the salt and sugar, then remove from the heat. Let cool for 10 minutes.

Meanwhile, put the chopped carrots in a large saucepan, cover with boiling water, add a pinch of salt, and boil for 2 minutes until just tender. Drain under running cold water to stop the cooking process and set aside.

Pack the carrots into sterilized 10-fl oz (300-ml) jars (see page 26) and cover with the cooled pickling liquid, leaving a 1-inch (2-cm) head space.

Allow the jars to stand uncovered, until the liquid cools completely, then cover the jars with the lids and store in a cool, dark place for up to 2 months. Wait a week before eating with the Zucchini Kuku (see page 120), or any of the savory Manoushe (see pages 188–193).

Turmeric-Pickled Cauliflower

PREPARATION TIME
10 minutes + 10 minutes cooling + 1 week standing time

COOKING TIME
10 minutes

MAKES
3 or 4 (8-fl oz/250-ml) jars

juice of 1 lemon
1 cup (8 fl oz/250 ml) white wine vinegar
1 tablespoon black mustard seeds
1 tablespoon celery seeds (optional)
1 tablespoon coriander seeds
1 stick cinnamon
2 tablespoons coarse sea salt
2 tablespoons golden superfine (caster) sugar
1 2-inch (5-cm) piece fresh turmeric, peeled and finely chopped
1 small head cauliflower (about 1 lb/450 g)

Pickles are enjoying a renaissance. When I was a young girl, they were a necessary bridge between the glut of late summer to the less abundant winter, but now they are cropping up on the menus of the most exciting restaurants. Pickles are an easy way to add lots of interesting flavor and texture, so I always like to have a few colorful jars in my larder.

I love pickling vegetables like this because it reminds me of a time when we would stretch the fresh produce to last for longer. Now, of course, it's very trendy. If you can get hold of celery seeds, do use them, they add such an interesting dimension to this pickle. You may wish to wear disposable or clean washing-up gloves when peeling and chopping the turmeric because it can stain your hands yellow for days.

PREPARATION

Put all the ingredients except the cauliflower in a large saucepan set over a medium-low heat and pour in 1 cup (8 fl oz/250 ml) water. Bring slowly to the boil.

Meanwhile, remove the outer leaves from the cauliflower and break the head into little florets, about the size of cherry tomatoes. You could use a knife to chop it up, if you find that easier, but you won't be left with the whole florets that look so pretty in the jar.

Once the pickling liquid has come to the boil, add the cauliflower florets, bring to the boil again, then remove from the heat and allow to cool for 10 minutes before carefully pouring into sterilized 8-fl oz (250-ml) jars (see page 26), leaving a 1-inch (2-cm) head space.

Allow the jars to stand uncovered, until the liquid cools completely, then cover the jars with lids and wait a week before eating. Store in a cool, dark place for up to 3 months.

Preserved Lemon Dressing

PREPARATION TIME	COOKING TIME	MAKES
10 minutes	–	scant 1 cup (7 fl oz/200 ml)

1 Preserved Lemon (see page 26)
1 small bunch mint, leaves finely chopped
1 small bunch parsley, leaves finely chopped
1 red chile, seeded and finely chopped
scant ½ cup (3 ½ fl oz/100 ml) olive oil
juice of 1 lemon
sea salt, to taste

See pages 22–23 for image

I like to serve this drizzled over very ripe tomatoes or to liven up baked rice with vegetables.

PREPARATION
Scrape away the flesh and pith from the preserved lemon rind and discard. Chop the rind as finely as you can with the herbs and chile, folding the mixture over itself on the board a few times with your knife.

Transfer the finely chopped herb and lemon mixture to a small bowl and mix with the oil and lemon juice. Add sea salt to taste.

Yogurt and Lemon Zest Dressing

PREPARATION TIME
10 minutes

COOKING TIME
–

MAKES
scant 1 cup (7 fl oz/200 ml)

⅔ cup (5 fl oz/150 ml) plain yogurt
zest and juice of ½ lemon
1 small bunch mint, leaves coarsely chopped
1 teaspoon honey
pinch of salt
cracked black pepper, to taste

See pages 22–23 for image

A quick and zesty dressing; as delicious on steamed greens as it is served with roast chicken.

PREPARATION
Combine all the ingredients in a bowl. Serve over steamed spring greens, purple sprouting broccoli, or kale.

1. Spicy Tahini Dressing (p.24) 2. Preserved Lemon Dressing (p.20) 3. Olive, Lemon, and Dill Dressing (p.25) 4. Yogurt and Lemon Zest Dressing (p.21)

Spicy Tahini Dressing

PREPARATION TIME
5 minutes

COOKING TIME
5 minutes

MAKES
scant 1 cup (7 fl oz/200 ml)

⅓ cup (2 ¾ oz/70 g) Tahini (see page 12)
juice of 1 lemon
1 tablespoon olive oil
3 garlic cloves, finely chopped
1 red chile, seeded and finely chopped
½ teaspoon cayenne pepper
3 tablespoons pine nuts
2 tablespoons toasted chopped walnuts
1 small bunch cilantro (coriander), leaves chopped

See pages 22–23 for image

This is delicious drizzled over roasted squash.

PREPARATION

Whisk the tahini and lemon juice together in a small bowl.

Heat the oil in a small skillet or frying pan over medium heat, add the garlic, chile, and cayenne pepper and fry for 1 minute until fragrant. Stir in the nuts and the tahini mixture, add 2–3 tablespoons water, then turn the heat down. Cook for 3 minutes until slightly thickened, then remove from the heat and immediately stir in the chopped cilantro (coriander).

If your tahini curdles, put the whole mixture into a blender, add a little warm water, and process to bring it together.

Olive, Lemon, and Dill Dressing

PREPARATION TIME
10 minutes

COOKING TIME
—

MAKES
scant 1 cup (7 fl oz/200 ml)

¼ cup (1 oz/25 g) green olives, pitted and halved lengthwise
zest and juice of 1 lemon
2 sprigs of dill, leaves only
⅓ cup (2 ½ fl oz/75 ml) olive oil
1 tablespoon cider vinegar
½ teaspoon soft brown sugar
generous pinch of salt
½ teaspoon toasted cumin seeds

See pages 22–23 for image

This is a dressing with a little more texture; try it with broiled (grilled) fish or bell peppers and zucchini (courgettes).

PREPARATION
Combine all the ingredients in a bowl. Serve over a simple green salad or sweet slow-roasted vegetables.

Preserved Lemons with Bay and Cinnamon

PREPARATION TIME
20 minutes +
overnight standing +
1 month standing time

COOKING TIME
—

MAKES
1 (1¾-pint/1-liter) jar

12 unwaxed lemons (6 washed, dried and stems removed; 6 juiced)
6 tablespoons coarse sea salt
6 bay leaves
2 tablespoons black peppercorns
1 cinnamon stick

Preserving lemons is very easy, using the natural acidity in lemon juice and the preserving power of salt to make them last. It's only the rind that you eat in the end; the juicy flesh of preserved lemons takes on so much salt that it is unpleasant to eat, whereas the oils in the rind (or skin) of the lemons preserve the natural aroma.

Chop the rind very finely, discard the flesh, and toss through salads, add to roasted veg, or stir through couscous. Preserved lemon is also delicious in stews or with olives.

STERILIZING JARS
Heat the oven to 275°F/140°C/Gas Mark 1. Wash the jars in hot soapy water, rinse, and dry well. Place in the center of the oven on a roasting tray for 10–15 minutes. Allow to cool completely before filling.

PREPARATION
Sterilize the preserving jar following the instructions given above.

Cut a deep cross in each of the 6 lemons, stopping ½–1 inch/1–2 cm from the tip, leaving the quarters attached at the end. Pinch the uncut end of the lemons to open up the quarters like a flower, before stuffing each with 1 tablespoon salt, 1 bay leaf, and a sprinkle of peppercorns. Do this over a bowl or over the jar so that any escaped salt can be rescued and added back into the jar. Add the cinnamon stick to the jar and push the lemons down into the jar as you go, packing them as tightly as possible. Pour over the lemon juice. Push the lemons back down so they are mostly covered with the juice, cover with the lid, and let stand overnight.

The next day, the lemons will have softened slightly and can be pushed down again to ensure they are fully submerged in the juice.

Keep in a cool place for at least 1 month and up to 3 months before eating. When ready, the lemons should be a yellow-brown color. Scrape away the flesh and pith and use the lemon rind only. Keep refrigerated once opened and consume within 3 months.

Fig and Rose Jam

PREPARATION TIME
10 minutes + resting

COOKING TIME
30 minutes

MAKES
2 or 3 (10-fl oz/300-ml) jars

2 ¼ lb/1 kg ripe figs (about 18)
½ cup (3 ½ oz/100 g) granulated sugar
zest of ½ orange
pinch of ground cinnamon
pinch of ground coriander
1 teaspoon rosewater (optional)
juice of ½ lemon
few sprigs of thyme
¼ cup (2 fl oz/50 ml) white wine

Figs are such a delicious fruit, but unfortunately their season isn't long. I make this jam at the beginning of autumn when the figs are at their best after they've had all summer to ripen in the sun. This jam is versatile; stir it through yogurt for breakfast, or use it as the filling in a sponge cake instead of raspberry or strawberry jam.

PREPARATION
Chop the figs into rough ½-inch/1-cm cubes and toss in a bowl with the sugar, orange zest, and ground spices. Set aside for 30 minutes.

Put the figs in a saucepan with the rosewater (if using), lemon juice, thyme, white wine, and 2 tablespoons water. Place over a medium heat and bring to a gentle simmer. Continue to gently simmer for 30 minutes, occasionally stirring with a wooden spoon, until the figs have shrunk and the liquid has thickened and reduced by a third. Remove the thyme sprigs.

Allow the jam to cool for 10 minutes before spooning into sterilized 10-fl oz (300-ml) jars (see page 26), leaving a 1-inch (2-cm) head space. When the jam is completely cool, screw on the lids. Store in the refrigerator for up to 1 month.

CHAPTER TWO

Dips & Nibbles

Babaganoush

PREPARATION TIME	COOKING TIME	SERVES
10 minutes + cooling time	30–45 minutes	4–6

3 eggplants (aubergines)
2 small garlic cloves
2 tablespoons Tahini (see page 12)
juice of ½ lemon
1 tablespoon olive oil
handful of pomegranate seeds, for sprinkling
salt and pepper

See pages 34–35 for image

For anyone who thinks they don't like eggplant (aubergine), I implore you to try this deliciously smoky, garlicky dip. The tahini adds a rich and creamy nuttiness to this Middle Eastern classic.

I like to let the babaganoush sit for half an hour or so to allow the flavors to mingle before diving in with toasted pita breads.

PREPARATION
Preheat the oven to 400°F/200°C/Gas Mark 6.

Put the eggplant (aubergines) onto a baking sheet, prick them all over with a fork, then roast in the oven for 30–45 minutes, until soft. Set aside to cool a little.

When cool enough to handle, peel off the skin and discard. Roughly chop the flesh and place it in a colander to drain, and allow the flesh to cool completely.

Put the garlic into a mortar with a little salt and crush with the pestle, then add the tahini and lemon juice, and mix well.

When the eggplant flesh is cool, chop it finely, transfer to a bowl, and add the garlic-tahini mixture. Season well and thoroughly combine all the ingredients. Place on a serving plate, then drizzle with olive oil and sprinkle over the pomegranate seeds.

Tahini and Grape Molasses Dip

PREPARATION TIME	COOKING TIME	SERVES
5 minutes	—	4

8 tablespoons Tahini (see page 12)
2–3 small garlic cloves, peeled
juice of 1 lemon
1 teaspoon Za'atar (see page 13)
1 teaspoon grape molasses
drizzle of olive oil
handful of soft herb leaves (I use dill, mint and parsley), to serve
salt and pepper

See pages 34–35 for image

As a young girl growing up, I used to wait for it to snow so I could mix it with grape molasses to make a slushie. Iron-rich grape molasses isn't as sharp as the more common pomegranate molasses, and it was used as a natural sweetener in Lebanon before white sugar was widely available. If you can't find grape molasses, try using a small amount of date molasses.

PREPARATION

Add 8 tablespoons lukewarm water to a food processor, then add the tahini, garlic, and lemon juice and process until light and fluffy. Add a little more water, if liked. Check seasoning, adding salt and pepper to taste.

Transfer the dip to a serving bowl and sprinkle over the za'atar. Spoon over the grape molasses and olive oil, then serve with fresh herbs scattered over the top.

34 BASICS

1. Tahini and Grape Molasses Dip (p.33) 2. Pickled Peppers Stuffed with Feta (p.37) 3. Lemon Artichoke Dip (p.36) 4. Babaganoush (p.32)

Lemon Artichoke Dip

PREPARATION TIME
5 minutes

COOKING TIME
5 minutes

SERVES
6

1 (11-oz/300-g) jar preserved artichokes (in oil or water is fine), drained
1 small bunch parsley, leaves only
1 tablespoon Tahini (see page 12)
3 tablespoons olive oil
zest and juice of 1 lemon (or more to taste)
2 small garlic cloves, peeled
salt and pepper

See pages 34–35 for image

Lemon and artichoke is a favorite flavor combination of mine. Whilst I love the flavor of freshly prepared artichoke leaves dipped in melted butter, sometimes time is short and I turn to the jarred variety to satisfy the craving. I like jarred artichokes preserved in oil, rather than brine.

PREPARATION
Blend all the ingredients in a food processor, until a rough paste forms. You want to still be able to see flecks of parsley, so stop regularly to scrape down the sides and process again.

Slowly add 3–5 tablespoons cold water, until the dip turns a lighter color and starts to look fluffier. Taste and add salt, pepper, and more lemon juice, if you like.

Pickled Peppers Stuffed with Feta

PREPARATION TIME
30 minutes + 1 hour cooling

COOKING TIME
15 minutes

MAKES
1 (34-fl oz/1-liter) jar or
2 (17-fl oz/500 ml) jars

11 oz/300 g mixed baby pimiento or cherry peppers
scant 1 cup (7 fl oz/200 ml) white wine vinegar
scant ½ cup (3 ½ fl oz/100 ml) olive oil, plus 1 ¼ cups (10 fl oz/300 ml) for bottling
1 tablespoon superfine (caster) sugar
6 black peppercorns
1 red chile, halved
1 garlic clove, peeled
7 oz/200 g feta cheese
1 ½ teaspoons dried mint
zest of 1 lemon

See pages 34–35 for image

This recipe really needs mini or baby chile peppers to work—I like pimiento or cherry peppers. The ratio of feta cheese to pepper should be quite balanced as the feta is so salty; anything too large will have an overpowering flavor and will be fiddly to eat.

PREPARATION

Slice the tips off the peppers, then scoop out the seeds and any white membrane from the sides with a small sharp knife or teaspoon. Don't worry about leaving a little—you don't want the peppers to break.

Put the peppers into a saucepan and pour over the vinegar, oil, and enough water to cover. Add the sugar, peppercorns, chile, and garlic, then simmer gently for 15 minutes over medium-low heat—don't let the mixture boil. Remove from the heat and let cool in the pickling liquid for 1 hour.

Meanwhile, mash the feta cheese in a bowl with a fork, then mix in the dried mint and lemon zest until smooth.

When completely cold, remove the peppers from the pickling liquid and dry on paper towels. Stuff the cavities of the peppers with the feta mixture, then put into sterilized jars (see page 26), cover with olive oil, seal, and store in the refrigerator for up to 1 month.

Roasted Baby Beets with Za'atar Labneh

PREPARATION TIME
15 minutes

COOKING TIME
40–90 minutes

SERVES
4

14 oz/400 g raw baby beets (beetroot) or regular beets, unpeeled and scrubbed
balsamic vinegar, for drizzling
olive oil, for drizzling
1 x quantity Labneh (see page 10), or thick Greek yogurt
2 tablespoons Za'atar (see page 13)
salt and pepper

Roasting beets (beetroot) with balsamic vinegar marinates the beets as they cook, mellowing the intense, earthy flavor. You could just as easily use larger beets, just give them about 20 minutes longer in the oven.

PREPARATION
Preheat the oven to 400°F/200°C/Gas Mark 6.

If the beets (beetroot) have leaves, remove them, discarding any really large or damaged ones, wash, and set aside.

Wrap each beet (beetroot) in aluminum foil with a splash of balsamic vinegar, olive oil, and a crack of salt and pepper. Place the little parcels in a roasting pan and roast in the oven for 30–40 minutes (for baby beets), or up to 90 minutes (for regular beets), until a sharp knife passes through the beets easily. When the beets are cooked, leave the oven on and spread the leaves on a baking sheet, leaving no overlap. Drizzle with olive oil and sprinkle with salt and pepper and place in the hot oven for 8 minutes until they're crisp and deep green.

Once cooked, remove the beets from the oven and peel away the foil from the cooked beets to let the steam escape. Set aside until cool enough to handle, then rub off the skins under cold running water and halve, quarter, or coarsely chop depending on the size.

Spread the labneh on a serving platter and sprinkle over the za'atar. Scatter the chopped beets over and drizzle more olive oil over the top, to serve.

Muhammara

PREPARATION TIME
10 minutes

COOKING TIME
30 minutes

SERVES
4–6

3 red bell peppers, seeded and cut into strips
olive oil, to drizzle
½ Arabic flatbread (or Pita Bread, see page 200)
½ teaspoon cayenne pepper
½ teaspoon smoked chili powder
1 ¼ cups (5 oz/150 g) chopped walnuts
1 tablespoon pomegranate molasses
juice of ½ lemon
1 tablespoon plain yogurt
1 tablespoon chopped parsley
2 tablespoons pine nuts, soaked in water for 20 minutes, then drained
salt and pepper
Pita Bread (see page 200), and remaining ½ Arabic flatbread to serve

See pages 42–43 for image

A little of this goes a long way; it's a richly textured and flavored dip from a combination of buttery walnuts, sharp pomegranate molasses, and sweet, smoky peppers.

As well as scooping onto pita breads, I also like to spread this muhammara in sandwiches with crisp lettuce, avocado, and broiled (grilled) halloumi for a quick and indulgent lunch for one, or more.

PREPARATION

Preheat the oven to 400°F/200°C/Gas Mark 6.

Place the strips of bell pepper on a baking sheet and lightly drizzle with olive oil. Roast for about 30 minutes until soft. Remove from the oven, put into a bowl, and cover with plastic wrap (clingfilm).

Meanwhile, put the flatbread on another baking sheet and bake for 5 minutes until golden and crisp. Transfer to a food processor and process to fine breadcrumbs. Transfer the breadcrumbs to a bowl, mix with the cayenne pepper and season well with salt and pepper. Set aside 1 tablespoon of breadcrumbs for garnish.

Pour a scant ½ cup (3 ½ fl oz/100 ml) water into the food processor and add the roasted peppers, spiced breadcrumbs, chili powder, walnuts, pomegranate molasses, and lemon juice. Pulse until the mixture is fine.

Transfer the muhammara to a bowl. Season with salt and pepper, stir in the yogurt, and sprinkle with chopped parsley, and pine nuts. Top with the reserved spiced breadcrumbs and serve with toasted pita bread.

Spiced Chickpea Popcorn

PREPARATION TIME	COOKING TIME	SERVES
5 minutes	25 minutes	4

1 (14-oz/400-g) can chickpeas, drained
3 tablespoons chickpea (gram) flour
½ teaspoon hot smoked paprika
generous pinch of salt
3 tablespoons vegetable oil
zest of ½ lemon, to serve
pinch of flaky sea salt, to serve

See pages 42–43 for image

I love making these to serve with drinks as an alternative to popcorn to whet the appetite before a mezze spread. They are slightly spicy, smoky, and salty, and incredibly easy to prepare.

PREPARATION
Preheat the oven to 425°F/220°C/Gas Mark 7. Line a baking sheet with parchment (baking) paper.
   Spread the chickpeas in an even layer on paper towels to dry them out as much as possible.
   Mix the chickpea (gram) flour, paprika, salt, and vegetable oil in a medium bowl and add the chickpeas, tossing to coat. Spread the chickpeas in an even layer on the lined baking sheet.
   Roast in the oven for 25 minutes, turning every 5 minutes or so until the chickpeas are so crispy you can hear them starting to pop.
   Serve while still warm with lemon zest and flaky sea salt sprinkled over the top.

1. Spiced Chickpea Popcorn (p.41) 2. Classic Hummus (p.45) 3. Muhammara (p.40) 4. Classic Falafel (p.44)

Classic Falafel

PREPARATION TIME
15 minutes + 1 overnight soaking + resting time

COOKING TIME
30 minutes

MAKES
20 falafel

generous 1 cup (7 oz/200 g) dried chickpeas
1 teaspoon baking soda (bicarbonate of soda), split
3 garlic cloves, peeled
1 small onion
1 tablespoon chopped cilantro (coriander)
1 tablespoon chopped parsley
1 tablespoon ground cumin
½ teaspoon dried mint
1 teaspoon ground coriander
1 x quantity Tahini (see page 12)
vegetable oil, for frying
salt

See pages 42–43 for image

A mezze just doesn't seem complete without falafel. I've been making them with the same ingredients since I can remember in spite of moving countries from Lebanon to England. I have to say though that the food processor makes quicker work of them than when I first made them.

PREPARATION

Soak the chickpeas overnight in plenty of water with ½ teaspoon baking soda (bicarbonate of soda).

The next day, drain the chickpeas well and discard any skins. Put the chickpeas, 2 garlic cloves, onion, cilantro (coriander), parsley, cumin, dried mint, ground coriander, and remaining baking soda into a food processor and process until smooth and thoroughly combined. Transfer the mixture to a bowl and press down with the back of a spoon. Cover the bowl with plastic wrap (clingfilm) and chill in the refrigerator for a few hours or overnight.

Using a falafel scoop, make 20 falafel, rinsing the scoop each time with hot water. If you don't have a scoop, take walnut-sized pieces of the mixture and shape them into small oval patties with damp hands.

Grate the remaining garlic clove. In a small bowl, combine the tahini and grated garlic, then season with salt and set aside.

Pour the vegetable oil into a saucepan to a depth of 4 inches/10 cm. Heat the oil to 350°F/180°C, or until a cube of bread browns in 30 seconds.

Working in batches, carefully fry the falafel for 1–2 minutes until golden. Make sure the oil is brought back up to temperature between batches. Remove the falafel with a slotted spoon and drain on paper towels.

Serve hot, drizzled with the tahini sauce.

Classic Hummus

PREPARATION TIME	COOKING TIME	SERVES
5 minutes	–	6

2 (14-oz/400-g) cans chickpeas
3 garlic cloves, coarsely chopped
4 tablespoons Tahini (see page 12)
juice of 2 lemons, or more to taste
2 teaspoons sea salt
extra virgin olive oil, for drizzling

See pages 42–43 for image

Probably the most famous and widely eaten Middle Eastern dip there is. I always like to have a bowl of hummus in the refrigerator to snack on, or in case family or friends come round unexpectedly. It's healthy, nourishing, and quickly comes together, which is perfect for busy gatherings.

PREPARATION
Drain the chickpeas, reserving scant ¼ cup (2 fl oz/50 ml) of liquid from the can. Put the chickpeas and liquid into a food processor with all the other ingredients and process until smooth. Add extra lemon juice according to taste.

Transfer into a dish and serve with a good drizzle of olive oil.

Little Damascus Kibbeh with Pine Nuts

PREPARATION TIME
50 minutes + 30 minutes chilling

COOKING TIME
30–40 minutes

MAKES
12 kibbeh

FOR THE SHELL
- 3 potatoes, peeled and finely diced
- 1 cup (7 oz/200 g) farina (coarse semolina)
- 1 ½ cups (11 oz/300 g) fine bulgur wheat
- 1 small bunch parsley, leaves chopped
- 1 small bunch cilantro (coriander), leaves chopped
- 1 onion, finely chopped
- ½ teaspoon pepper
- 1 teaspoon ground cumin
- 1 teaspoon Lebanese 7-Spice Seasoning (see page 12)
- vegetable oil, for deep-frying

FOR THE STUFFING
- 1 tablespoon olive oil
- 1 onion, finely chopped
- ¼ teaspoon pepper
- ¼ teaspoon Lebanese 7-Spice Seasoning (see page 12)
- 2 small potatoes, peeled and finely diced
- ½ cup (2 oz/50 g) pine nuts
- sea salt

FOR THE SAUCE
- 1 onion, finely chopped
- 3 garlic cloves, chopped
- olive oil, for frying
- ½ teaspoon ground cumin
- 1 teaspoon salt
- ½ teaspoon pepper
- 1 tablespoon all-purpose (plain) flour
- scant ½ cup (3 ½ oz/100 g) tomato paste (purée)

My grandchildren love this incidentally vegan kibbeh, which I shape into pointed ovals. When they cook, the shell turns deeply crispy and the filling stays soft and nourishing, almost like a stuffing.

PREPARATION

For the kibbeh shell, boil the potatoes in salted water until tender. Drain, then return to the saucepan over low heat to dry them out. Mash and season well, then let cool until easy to handle.

In a bowl, combine the farina (coarse semolina) and enough lukewarm water to just cover it. Soak for 20 minutes. Meanwhile, rinse the bulgur wheat, then drain both in a fine strainer (sieve).

Combine all the kibbeh shell ingredients, except the oil, in a bowl and mix with your hands to bring everything together like a dough. Cover and let rest in the refrigerator for 30 minutes.

Meanwhile, to make the stuffing, heat the oil in a skillet or frying pan over medium heat and sauté the onion for 10–12 minutes, until softened. Stir in the pepper and spice, then add the potatoes and pine nuts, season well, and cook for 15–20 minutes, until just cooked. Stir occasionally.

Take golf-ball sized portions of the chilled kibbeh shell mixture and use your hands to form a lemon-shaped oval. Push a finger into the ball (not right through) to form a hole in the middle and fill with a teaspoon of the stuffing. Seal the hole with a pinch. Alternatively, with wet hands, flatten the mixture into a disk, then mold it around a teaspoon of the filling. Repeat with the rest of the mixture to make 12 kibbeh. They can be frozen at this stage (defrost thoroughly before cooking).

Pour the vegetable oil for deep-frying into a large, deep saucepan, to a depth of 1 ½–2 inches/4–5 cm, and set over medium heat. For best results, deep-fry the kibbeh at 325–350°F/170–180°C for 5–8 minutes, or until golden. (If you don't have a cooking thermometer, drop a little of the mixture into the oil—if the oil is hot enough, it should brown and rise to the surface.) Use a slotted spoon to carefully lower the kibbeh into the oil and cook in small batches of 4 or 5 at a time. Drain on paper towels and keep warm.

To make the sauce, cook the onion and garlic in a little olive oil over medium heat for 10–12 minutes. Add the cumin, salt, pepper, and flour, followed by the tomato paste (purée), and scant 1 cup (7 fl oz/200 ml) water. Simmer for 10 minutes, or until slightly thickened. Serve in bowls with the sauce as the base and the warm kibbeh resting on top of the sauce, so the kibbeh stay crispy.

Crispy Artichoke Hearts with Za'atar Aioli

PREPARATION TIME
10 minutes

COOKING TIME
4–6 minutes

SERVES
4–6

12 artichoke hearts (from a can or jar), halved if small or quartered if large

FOR THE ZA'ATAR AIOLI
1 small garlic clove
pinch of salt
1 egg yolk
1 tablespoon Dijon mustard
1 ¼ cups (10 fl oz/300 ml) extra virgin olive oil
scant 1 cup (7 fl oz/200ml) mild olive oil
lemon juice, to taste
salt and pepper
1 teaspoon Za'atar (see page 13)
lemon wedges, to serve (optional)

See pages 50–51 for image

I find this easiest to make with canned or jarred artichokes, but you could also use globe artichokes when in season, although they are a bit fiddly to prepare.

PREPARATION
For the aioli, finely chop the garlic with a pinch of salt, rolling the side of the knife over the garlic repeatedly to crush it and work the salt in, to make a paste.

In a large mixing bowl, whisk the egg yolk together with the Dijon mustard, then slowly pour in the extra virgin olive oil, whisking all the time. When the mixture starts to thicken, you can start to add the milder olive oil more quickly. When you have reached a mayonnaise-like consistency, add the lemon juice to taste, the garlic paste, and some salt and pepper. Sprinkle with the za'atar and set aside until you're ready to eat.

Set a ridged grill (griddle) pan over high heat. As soon as the grill pan is really hot (it should have been heated for at least 3 minutes), arrange the artichoke hearts on the pan in a single layer, without overcrowding the pan. Cook for 2–3 minutes on each side, until they start to char.

Serve the artichoke hearts alongside the aioli, with more lemon wedges for squeezing over, if you like.

Preserved Lemon and Bay-Scented Olives

PREPARATION TIME
10 minutes

COOKING TIME
—

MAKES
1 (14-fl oz/400-ml) jar

2 ½ cups (9 oz/250 g) pitted Kalamata and Spanish queen (green) olives in brine (drained weight)
½ Preserved Lemon (see page 26)
2 or 3 bay leaves
4 tablespoons olive oil

See pages 50–51 for image

Buttery olives are a brilliant addition to any mezze spread. I like to flavor my own olives as I find the individual taste of each ingredient is so much stronger.

PREPARATION
Drain, then thoroughly rinse the olives to remove the brine. Cut a small cross into the base of each and put into a bowl.

Drain and rinse the preserved lemon half, then scrape off and discard the flesh. Chop the rind finely and add it to the bowl, along with the bay leaves and olive oil. Mix thoroughly.

Store in a sterilized jar (see page 26) in the refrigerator for up to 6 weeks, turning from time to time to mix the ingredients.

Remove from the refrigerator at least 15 minutes before serving to allow the dressing to liquefy.

1. Crispy Artichoke Hearts with Za'atar Aioli (p.48)

2. Orange, Rosemary, and Coriander Olives (p.52) 3. Preserved Lemon and Bay-Scented Olives (p.49) 4. Seeded Pomegranate Olives (p.53)

Orange, Rosemary, and Coriander Olives

PREPARATION TIME
10 minutes

COOKING TIME
—

MAKES
1 (14-fl oz/400-ml) jar

2 ½ cups (9 oz/250 g) pitted Kalamata and Spanish queen (green) olives in brine (drained weight)
zest and juice of ½ orange
4 tablespoons olive oil
few sprigs of rosemary
1 teaspoon coriander seeds

See pages 50–51 for image

PREPARATION
Drain, then thoroughly rinse the olives to remove the brine. Cut a small cross into the base of each and put into a bowl.

Cut the orange zest into long, thin strips and add to the bowl, along with the orange juice, olive oil, and rosemary. Crush the coriander seeds in a pestle and mortar and add them to the bowl. Mix thoroughly.

Store in a sterilized jar (see page 26) in the refrigerator for up to 6 weeks, turning from time to time to mix the ingredients.

Remove from the refrigerator at least 15 minutes before serving to allow the dressing to liquefy.

Seeded Pomegranate Olives

PREPARATION TIME
10 minutes

COOKING TIME
–

MAKES
1 (14-fl oz/400-ml) jar

2 ½ cups (9 oz/250 g) pitted Kalamata and Spanish queen (green) olives in brine (drained weight)
5 tablespoons pomegranate molasses
2 tablespoons olive oil
1 tablespoon Za'atar Toasted Seed Mix (see page 56), to serve

See pages 50–51 for image

PREPARATION
Drain, then thoroughly rinse the olives to remove the brine. Cut a small cross into the base of each and put into a bowl. Pour over the molasses and olive oil. Mix thoroughly.

When ready to serve, sprinkle over a handful of toasted seeds for some extra crunch. Store in a sterilized jar (see page 26) in the refrigerator for up to 6 weeks.

Remove from the refrigerator at least 15 minutes before serving to allow the dressing to liquefy.

Tomato and Chili Relish with Toasted Pita Chips

PREPARATION TIME
10 minutes

COOKING TIME
15 minutes

SERVES
4–6 as a light snack

olive oil, for frying
½ red onion, finely chopped
2 small garlic cloves, thinly sliced
6 large vine tomatoes, coarsely chopped
1 teaspoon pul biber (Turkish chili flakes)
½ teaspoon dried mint
salt

FOR THE PITA CHIPS
4 small Pita Breads (see page 200), torn into rough triangles about 1 inch/ 2.5 cm
olive oil
1 generous pinch of pul biber (Turkish chili flakes)
salt

Turkish chili flakes, or pul biber, are widely available in corner stores and specialist food stores, but for some reason are often difficult to find in supermarkets. They are less spicy than common dried chili flakes, but have a lovely flavor and are used widely beyond Turkey in Middle Eastern cooking.

PREPARATION
Preheat the oven to 400°F/200°C/Gas Mark 6.

Heat a splash of olive oil in a small saucepan, add the red onion and a pinch of salt and cook over medium heat for 4–5 minutes. Add the garlic and cook for 1 minute, before increasing the temperature slightly and adding the tomatoes, pul biber, dried mint, and salt, if needed. Cook for another 5–7 minutes, until the tomatoes have lost their moisture and the relish has thickened and reduced.

Meanwhile, arrange the pita pieces in one layer (without overlapping) over one or two baking sheets. Drizzle over a couple of glugs of olive oil to lightly coat, then season with pul biber and a pinch of salt. Place in the oven to crisp up for 5–7 minutes.

Serve the relish in a bowl, with the pita chips around the side for dipping.

Za'atar Toasted Seed Mix

PREPARATION TIME	COOKING TIME	SERVES
5 minutes	5–7 minutes	4–6

1 tablespoon extra-virgin olive oil
1 tablespoon Za'atar (see page 13)
1 teaspoon salt
7 oz/200 g mixed seeds (I like a combination of pumpkin seeds, sunflower seeds, sesame seeds and flax seeds/linseeds)

These crunchy seeds are a perfect starter to a mezze spread, but also add interest and flavor to salads and roasted root vegetables. I like to try different seeds and sometimes whole spices, to layer different flavors through the seeds.

PREPARATION
Preheat the oven to 350°F/180°C/Gas Mark 4.

Put the olive oil, za'atar, and salt into a bowl and mix until you have a paste, loosening with another drizzle of olive oil if needed. Stir the seeds through the paste until they are evenly covered.

Spread the seeds out in one layer (without overlapping) in a large roasting pan, ovenproof skillet or frying pan, then cook in the hot oven for 5–7 minutes until the seeds are lightly toasted. Drain on paper towels to remove any excess oil.

Store in an airtight container and eat within 6 weeks.

Hummus with Lamb and Pine Nuts

PREPARATION TIME
10 minutes

COOKING TIME
10 minutes

SERVES
6–8

2 (14-oz/400-g) cans chickpeas
3 garlic cloves, peeled
4 tablespoons Tahini (see page 12)
juice of 2 lemons
2 teaspoons sea salt
extra virgin olive oil, for drizzling
toasted flatbreads, to serve

FOR THE LAMB AND PINE NUT TOPPING
½ teaspoon olive oil
3 ½ oz/100 g ground (minced) lamb
¼ teaspoon Lebanese 7-Spice Seasoning (see page 12)
⅓ cup (1 ½ oz/40 g) pine nuts, toasted
salt and pepper

This dish is so quick to come together and the addition of warm-spiced lamb transforms this classic dip to one of the most satisfying and flavorsome Lebanese mezze dishes. What I love most about it is the moreish textural combination of light-as-air hummus and spicy, crisped-at-the-edges fried meat. Serve this simply with toasted flatbread.

PREPARATION
First, make the lamb and pine nut topping. Heat the oil in a skillet or frying pan, add the lamb, and cook over medium heat for 5–6 minutes until evenly browned. Add the spice seasoning and season to taste with salt and pepper. Stir in the toasted pine nuts and remove the pan from the heat.

Drain the chickpeas, reserving ¼ cup (2 fl oz/50 ml) of the can juices, and rinse. Put the chickpeas into a food processor, add the garlic cloves and tahini, and process for a few minutes. Add the reserved can juices, followed by half the lemon juice and the sea salt, and process until smooth. Taste and add more lemon juice, if you like. Scrape the hummus into a serving dish, drizzle generously with olive oil, top with the lamb and pine nuts, and serve with toasted flatbread.

Mini Flatbreads with Crab and Salmon

PREPARATION TIME
15 minutes

COOKING TIME
8–10 minutes

SERVES
2–4

2 small flatbreads
1 x 7 oz/200 g salmon fillet, skinned
7 oz/200g crabmeat
grated zest and juice of 1 lemon
1 tablespoon chopped chervil
1 tablespoon chopped parsley
1 tablespoon chopped cilantro (coriander)
½ teaspoon ground sumac
½ teaspoon cayenne pepper

FOR THE DRESSING
5 tablespoons plain (natural) yogurt
1 tablespoon Tahini (see page 12)
½ teaspoon tomato paste (purée)
1 tablespoon lemon juice
salt and pepper

TO SERVE
cayenne pepper
watercress
¼ teaspoon black sesame seeds

See pages 62–63 for image

The combination of crab and fresh herbs just tastes like summer to me. I love the delicate aniseed flavor of cilantro (coriander) and chervil when scattered over the sweet shellfish. These mini flatbreads look very sophisticated handed round before a summer BBQ. I recommend serving them alongside the lamb and anchovy flatbreads (see opposite) for a salty contrast. I like to use flatbreads which look like rounded pita breads. Just be sure to griddle them for a couple of minutes on each side to warm up and impart a slightly smoky flavor.

PREPARATION
Heat a ridged grill (griddle) pan and, when it is hot, add the flatbreads. Warm through, turning once, until lightly charred on both sides. Set aside and keep warm.

Heat a pan of water just to boiling point, reduce the heat so that the surface is barely simmering, add the salmon fillet, and poach for 7–8 minutes.

Transfer the fish to a plate with a slotted spatula (fish slice) and let cool, then flake into large pieces and put in a bowl. Add the crabmeat, lemon juice, herbs, sumac, and cayenne pepper and mix gently. Mix together all the dressing ingredients in a bowl and season to taste with salt and pepper.

Spoon the crab and salmon mixture onto the warm flatbreads, drizzle with the dressing, and garnish with a pinch of cayenne pepper, watercress, lemon zest, and black sesame seeds.

Mini Flatbreads with Lamb and Anchovies

PREPARATION TIME
15 minutes

COOKING TIME
40 minutes

SERVES
2–4

2 small flatbreads
½ teaspoon olive oil
7 oz/200 g ground (minced) lamb
1 small onion, chopped
3 canned anchovies, drained and finely chopped
1 teaspoon Lebanese 7-Spice Seasoning (see page 12)
1 teaspoon ground cumin
½ teaspoon ground cinnamon
¼ teaspoon ground allspice
3 tablespoons chopped mint
juice of ½ lemon
salt and pepper

FOR THE DRESSING
3 tablespoons plain (natural) yogurt
1 teaspoon grated lemon zest
1 tablespoon chopped mint
pepper

See pages 62–63 for image

I like to think of these as individual Turkish-style pizzas. They make for a quick and delicious supper to have with friends, or as part of a larger mezze spread before a summer BBQ along with the mini flatbreads topped with crab, salmon, and tahini dressing (see opposite).

In spite of its small size, anchovy packs a powerful punch in terms of flavor and seasoning capability. In this recipe, I cook it down slowly with the lamb to melt into the Middle Eastern-spiced flatbread topping. If you think you don't really like fish, I implore you to try this way with anchovies, which only supports the flavor of the lamb, rather than overpowering it.

PREPARATION
Heat a ridged grill (griddle) pan and, when it is hot, add the flatbreads. Warm through, turning once, until lightly charred on both sides. Set aside and keep warm.

Heat the oil in a non-stick skillet or frying pan, add the lamb, and cook over medium heat, stirring frequently, for 5–8 minutes until evenly browned. Add the onion and anchovies, reduce the heat to low, and cook, stirring occasionally, for another 10 minutes. Stir in all the spices, add a little water if the pan seems too dry, and simmer for 20 minutes. Stir in the mint and lemon juice and season with salt and pepper. Remove the pan from the heat. Mix together all the dressing ingredients in a small bowl and season with a pinch of pepper.

Spoon the lamb mixture onto the warm flatbreads and drizzle with the dressing.

1. Mini Flatbreads with Lamb and Anchovies (p.61) 2. Mini Flatbreads with Crab and Salmon (p.60)

CHAPTER THREE

Salads

Charred Cauliflower with Pickled Apple

PREPARATION TIME	COOKING TIME	SERVES
20 minutes	30 minutes	6 as small plates

FOR THE PICKLED APPLE
- 1 eating apple, cored and cut into matchsticks (no need to peel)
- 2 tablespoons white wine vinegar
- juice of 1 lemon
- ½ teaspoon fine sea salt
- ½ teaspoon golden superfine (caster) sugar

FOR THE CREAMED CHICKPEAS
- 3 tablespoons extra virgin olive oil
- 3 garlic cloves, finely chopped
- 1 teaspoon ground cumin
- 1 (14-oz/400-g) can chickpeas, drained and half the liquid reserved
- 1 bay leaf
- zest and juice of ½ lemon

FOR THE CAULIFLOWER
- 1 cauliflower, washed and cut into evenly sized florets
- 4 tablespoons olive oil
- 1 teaspoon fennel seeds
- salt and pepper
- 1 small bunch parsley, leaves picked and coarsely chopped, to serve

Roasting cauliflower really transforms this humble vegetable. I have a number of memories that I'd rather forget of eating overcooked cauliflower, either boiled or steamed, which tasted so sulfurous and underwhelming. Roasting (with its tender inner leaves as well) turns the cauliflower nutty rather than mushy.

PREPARATION
To pickle the apple, toss the chopped apple in a bowl with the vinegar, lemon juice, salt, and sugar, then top up with a little water to cover, pressing the apple down to make sure it is fully sumerged. Set aside. Preheat the oven to 400°F/200°C/Gas Mark 6.

Heat the olive oil in a small saucepan with a lid over medium heat. Add the garlic and stir-fry for 30 seconds, then add the cumin, chickpeas, reserved chickpea liquid, and bay leaf. Turn the heat down to low, cover the pan with the lid, and cook for 30 minutes, stirring occasionally.

Meanwhile, toss the cauliflower florets with the olive oil and fennel seeds until well coated. Arrange in one layer (without overlapping) in a roasting pan and roast in the oven for 20 minutes, until cooked through and charred in places. Season with salt and pepper while still warm.

When the chickpeas are cooked, add the lemon zest and juice, and season generously with salt and pepper. Briefly blitz with an immersion (stick) blender in different places around the pan so that you get some creamed chickpeas and some chickpeas with more texture in places.

Arrange the chickpeas on a large serving plate, top with the cauliflower, then scatter over the pickled apple and chopped parsley. Serve while still warm.

Green Bean and Hazelnut Salad

PREPARATION TIME	COOKING TIME	SERVES
20 minutes	5 minutes	2

¼ large cucumber
1 tablespoon white wine vinegar
juice of ½ lemon
½ teaspoon fine sea salt
½ teaspoon golden superfine (caster) sugar
11 oz/300 g fine green beans, trimmed
3 radishes
1 small bunch dill
¼ cup (1 oz/30 g) hazelnuts, toasted
salt and pepper

FOR THE DRESSING
1 tablespoon pomegranate molasses
½ teaspoon honey
2 tablespoons olive oil
zest and juice of ½ orange
pinch of allspice
salt and pepper

TO SERVE
1 oz/30 g feta cheese, crumbled (optional)

This green bean salad is a riot of color and texture: buttery from the toasted hazelnuts, vibrant from the herbs, with the sweet sharpness of pomegranate molasses. It's the kind of food I like to eat when it's too hot outside, because it requires minimal effort and is somehow deeply satisfying and cooling.

PREPARATION
First, pickle the cucumber. Slice the cucumber quarter down the middle, then scrape out the watery seeds with the tip of a teaspoon and discard. Cut the remaining cucumber into ½-inch/1-cm slices and put into a bowl with the vinegar, lemon juice, salt, and sugar. Mix with your hands to make sure each cucumber slice is covered in grains of salt and sugar.

Bring a large saucepan of water to the boil and add a generous pinch of salt. Add the fine green beans and boil for 4 minutes.

Meanwhile, in a small bowl combine the pomegranate molasses, honey, olive oil, orange zest and juice, allspice, and salt and pepper to taste.

Drain the beans and, while they are still warm, toss the dressing through them to allow the beans to take on the flavors. Let cool to room temperature before serving.

Slice the radishes into thin rounds, or half-moons if they are quite large, then toss through the cooled beans. Pick the dill from the stalks and mix through as well. Arrange the dressed beans on a platter, then roughly chop the hazelnuts and scatter over the top. Drain the pickled cucumbers and scatter over the top as well.

Serve with the feta cheese crumbled over, if using.

Winter Tabbouleh

PREPARATION TIME	COOKING TIME	SERVES
20 minutes + 5–10 minutes soaking time	—	6 as small plates

1 ¼ cups (7 oz/200 g) coarse bulgur wheat
1 cup (8 fl oz/250 ml) hot vegetable stock
1 red onion, finely diced
1 fennel bulb, thinly sliced
½ celery root (celeriac), peeled and sliced into thin strips
1 bunch parsley, finely chopped
1 bunch mint, finely chopped
⅔ cup (5 fl oz/150 ml) extra virgin olive oil
juice of 1 lemon
2 tablespoons pomegranate molasses
2 tablespoons pomegranate seeds
⅓ cup (2 oz/50 g) walnuts, coarsely chopped
salt and pepper

See pages 72–73 for image

Although it may taste like the sun, pomegranate is in fact in season at my adopted home in London around the same time as the winter citrus becomes available in the greengrocer, around January and February. It adds such a pop of flavor and brightness that when I'm eating this salad, I can almost feel the sun on my cheeks.

I use celery root (celeriac) and fennel here, which work well with the other flavors, and they're served raw, which I often crave at the beginning of the year after lots of rich food.

PREPARATION
Put the bulgur wheat into a bowl, pour the hot stock over it, cover, and let stand for 5–10 minutes, or until the liquid has been absorbed. Drain in a strainer (sieve) lined with cheesecloth (muslin), squeezing out as much liquid as possible. Put it into a bowl and fluff up the grains with a fork. Add the onion, fennel, and celery root (celeriac), mix well, then add the parsley and mint.

Whisk together the olive oil, lemon juice, and pomegranate molasses in a small bowl, season well, then pour the dressing over the tabbouleh. Sprinkle with the pomegranate seeds and chopped walnuts to serve.

Mograbieh (Giant Couscous) Salad

PREPARATION TIME
15 minutes

COOKING TIME
10 minutes

SERVES
6

1 ⅓ cups (7 oz/200 g) whole wheat mograbieh (giant couscous)
½ vegetable bouillon (stock) cube (optional)
4 vine tomatoes, diced
¼ cucumber, seeded and finely chopped

FOR THE DRESSING
1 Preserved Lemon (see page 26)
2 tablespoons olive oil
1 teaspoon toasted cumin seeds
½ red chile, seeded and finely sliced
handful of mixed soft herbs (such as dill, parsley, mint, tarragon and Greek basil), coarsely chopped
salt and pepper

See pages 72–73 for image

Giant couscous, or *mograbieh*, is made by gradually adding water to semolina and rolling it by hand to form pearls of dough, which are then dried. I find it more toothsome and nourishing than the more common couscous, and use whole wheat mograbieh where I can find it, which takes a little longer to cook.

PREPARATION
Cook the mograbieh (giant couscous) according to the packet directions. I like to add half a cube of vegetable bouillon (stock) to impart some flavor to the grains as they cook.

To make the dressing, scrape away the flesh and pith from the preserved lemon rind and discard. Chop the rind as finely as you can. In a small bowl, mix the chopped lemon rind with the olive oil, cumin seeds, and chile, then taste to check the seasoning, adding salt and pepper to taste. Stir in the chopped herbs.

Drain the mograbieh, arrange over a serving dish, mix with the chopped tomatoes and cucumber, and stir through the dressing while still warm.

2. Mograbieh (Giant Couscous) Salad (p.71) 3. Winter Tabbouleh (p.70) 4. Griddled Lettuce Salad with Crispy Chickpeas (p.75)

Rainbow Beet Salad with Walnut Pesto

PREPARATION TIME
30 minutes

COOKING TIME
—

SERVES
6–8

2 medium beets (beetroot), peeled
2 candy beets (beetroot), peeled
zest and juice of 2 limes
2 shallots, finely sliced
pinch of salt
pinch of superfine (caster) sugar
1 tablespoon white wine vinegar
1 orange

FOR THE WALNUT PESTO
1 small bunch parsley, with a few leaves reserved for garnish
2 Medjool dates, pitted
50 g walnuts
juice of ½ lemon
drizzle of olive oil (optional)
salt and pepper

See pages 72–73 for image

If you can get your hands on yellow beets (beetroot) or other colored beets, do swap these in place of the classic deep purple kind.

PREPARATION
Thinly slice the beets (beetroot) with a mandoline, then collect any odds and ends and slice them into thin matchsticks. Put the beets into a bowl with the lime juice and zest, and toss to combine. Set aside.

Put the shallots into a small mixing bowl with the salt, sugar, and vinegar, then scrunch well with your hands until you feel the shallots begin to soften. Set aside.

Pulse all the pesto ingredients in a food processor to a chunky paste—you don't want it too fine, a few larger walnut pieces add interesting texture to the salad. Taste to check the seasoning and make any adjustments you'd like—adding a drizzle of oil if desired.

When you're ready to serve, layer the beet slices and matchsticks on a platter. Cut a slice from the bottom of the orange so that it sits flat on the chopping board, then cut thick slices of peel from around the orange, removing all the pith. Keep any juicy slices aside, as you will use the juice later. The lines of the segments should now be visible; cut between them to pull out juicy segments of orange. Scatter the orange segments over the beets, then squeeze the juice from the offcuts over the top of the salad to season it.

Squeeze the pickling liquid from the shallots, then scatter over the salad with the reserved parsley leaves to garnish. Serve with the walnut pesto on the side.

Griddled Lettuce Salad with Crispy Chickpeas

PREPARATION TIME
15 minutes

COOKING TIME
20 minutes

SERVES
6–8 as small plates,
depending on size of lettuce

- 2 Boston or Little Gem lettuce, washed, dried, and quartered from top to bottom
- 2 tablespoons vegetable or sunflower oil
- 1 (14-oz/400-g) can chickpeas, drained and dried on paper towels
- ½ teaspoon smoked paprika
- ½ teaspoon chili powder
- ½ teaspoon cumin seeds
- 1 small bunch mint, leaves picked and coarsely chopped
- 1 small bunch parsley, leaves picked and coarsely chopped
- salt and pepper

FOR THE DRESSING
- 1 shallot, peeled and finely chopped
- 10 green olives, finely chopped
- 2 tablespoons Tahini (see page 12)
- 1 garlic clove, finely chopped
- zest and juice of 1 lemon

See pages 72–73 for image

If you don't have a ridged grill (griddle) pan, these lettuces work very well on a hot BBQ in the summer—just don't close the lid!

PREPARATION
Preheat the oven to 400°F/200°C/Gas Mark 6.

Heat a ridged grill (griddle) pan over the highest heat possible.

Add the oil to a small roasting pan and place in the oven for 3 minutes until really hot. Remove the pan from the oven, then toss the drained chickpeas in the pan with the spices, and some salt and pepper. Cook in the oven for 12–15 minutes, until they are starting to "pop" and have turned a warm russet color.

Meanwhile, use a fork to whisk together the dressing ingredients in a small bowl, adding 2 tablespoons of water. Depending on the tahini you're using, you may need to thin the dressing with a splash more water (you are looking for the consistency of thick pouring cream). Add salt and pepper to taste, remembering that the olives will be quite salty.

When ready to serve, grill the lettuce cut-side down for 2–3 minutes, until charred.

Arrange the lettuce halves on a serving platter and scatter over the warm chickpeas. Drizzle with the tahini dressing, then scatter the mint and parsley over the top.

Clementine Salad with Black Olives

PREPARATION TIME
15 minutes

COOKING TIME
5 minutes

SERVES
4–6 as small plates

3 tablespoons walnut oil
4 seedless clementines, halved around the middle
2 large oranges
20 pitted Kalamata olives, coarsely chopped
handful of mint, leaves only
flaky sea salt and pepper

Olives and oranges may sound like an unusual combination, but this dish has its roots in Morocco, where the two are ripened by the hot Middle Eastern sun.

Use Kalamata olives with smooth skins, rather than the wrinkly, dry black olives that are so salty, they'll overpower the other flavors.

I use walnut oil in this dish, but Moroccans would use Argan oil, which is also a brilliant treatment for hair.

PREPARATION

Heat 2 tablespoons of walnut oil in a small skillet or frying pan over medium heat. When the oil is hot, place the clementine halves cut-side down in the pan and cook for around 4 minutes, until the fruit is caramelized and sticky.

Meanwhile, cut the bottom off the oranges so that they sit flat on the board and use a sharp knife to cut the skin and membrane away, so that no white pith is visible, only the bright orange of the juicy fruit inside. Slice the oranges into the thinnest rounds you can, reserving any orange juice you can save (including any juicy bits from the skins you've cut away). Arrange the slices on a plate, picking out any visible pips as you go.

When the clementines are cooked, remove to a board to cool. Pour the reserved orange juice into the same pan with the remaining tablespoon of walnut oil and warm over low heat.

When the clementines are cool enough to handle, peel the skins away then tear into irregular pieces and scatter over the top of the orange slices, along with the chopped olives and mint leaves. Drizzle the warmed juice and walnut oil over the top, then season with salt and pepper. Let the salad sit for 15 minutes for the flavors to mingle before serving.

Tahini Rémoulade

PREPARATION TIME
25 minutes + 15 minutes standing time

COOKING TIME
—

SERVES
6 as small plates

1 celery root (celeriac)
1 eating apple
zest and juice of 1 lemon
4 tablespoons Tahini (see page 12)
3 tablespoons water
1 tablespoon olive oil
1 heaping teaspoon dried mint
splash of white wine or cider vinegar
salt and pepper

Celery root (celariac) rémoulade is a classic French dish, made with mayonnaise and crème fraîche. I've used tahini here, which is vegan and less cloying than the richer, classic version.

PREPARATION

Peel the celery root (celeriac) with a large, sharp knife then cut it into matchsticks. You may find it easiest to cut the celery root into quarters, lay one of the flat edges on your chopping board, then cut it into very thin slices. Layer 3–4 slices on top of each other, then cut into fine matchsticks. Alternatively, use the largest side of a box grater to coarsely grate the celery root. Peel, core, and grate the apple, or cut into fine slices. Put the celery root into a large mixing bowl with the apple, and immediately toss with the lemon juice, and a pinch of salt. Set aside while you get on with the dressing.

In a small bowl, whisk together the tahini, olive oil, dried mint, vinegar, lemon zest and 3 tablespoons of water. Season with salt and pepper. If the dressing looks as though it's separating, mix in another tablespoon or so of water, and stir to combine (you are looking for the consistency of thick pouring cream).

Transfer the celery root and apple to a large serving bowl, mix in the dressing, then let stand for at least 15 minutes before serving.

1. Cabbage and Apple Slaw (p.117) 2. Tahini Rémoulade (p.78)

Labneh with Figs and Candied Walnuts

PREPARATION TIME
10 minutes

COOKING TIME
5 minutes

SERVES
4

⅓ cup (1 ½ oz/40 g) walnuts, coarsely chopped
3 tablespoons superfine (caster) sugar
2 scant tablespoons (¾ oz/20 g) butter
pinch of salt
1 x quantity Labneh (see page 10)
8 figs, torn into quarters with your hands
handful of peppery salad leaves (I like to use arugula/rocket or watercress) or a mixture of both
1½ teaspoons balsamic vinegar (optional)
1 tablespoon olive oil (optional)

This is a brilliant dish to make when the figs are at their ripest, usually at the onset of autumn. Juicy and aromatic, they pair so well with the peppery leaves. I like to use a mixture of leaves to add lots of different tones of green to the salad. Be generous with the olive oil too, and use the best quality you can find.

PREPARATION

To make the candied walnuts, have a piece of parchment (baking) paper ready on a flat surface near your stove. Place the walnuts, sugar, and butter in a small skillet or frying pan over medium heat and stir continuously for 3–5 minutes, until the butter and sugar melt and the walnuts turn a deep golden color. Remove to the parchment paper and spread out, so that you have individual pieces of candied walnuts rather than one candied slab. Sprinkle with a pinch of salt and let set.

Spread the labneh on a serving platter, dot the quartered figs over the top and nestle the salad leaves around the platter too. Scatter the candied walnuts over the top and drizzle over a little balsamic vinegar and olive oil, if you like.

Cauliflower Couscous with Pine Nuts and Raisins

PREPARATION TIME
10 minutes

COOKING TIME
15 minutes

SERVES
4 as small plates

½ large cauliflower (about 1 lb 2 oz/500 g)
olive oil, for frying
⅔ cup (3 ½ oz/100 g) pine nuts
scant ½ cup (2 oz/50 g) golden raisins (Turkish sultanas) or any large juicy raisins
1 teaspoon dried mint
juice of ½ lemon
2 tablespoons extra virgin olive oil
1 shallot, finely chopped
pinch of salt, or more to taste
feta cheese, to serve (optional)

This is a brilliant gluten-free option to conventional couscous, and is light and delicious too.

If you want to serve this warm, simply add a splash of oil to the pan after you've toasted the pine nuts, stir the grated cauliflower through and cook over a medium heat for 4-5 minutes before adding the remaining ingredients.

PREPARATION

Coarsely grate the cauliflower, including the core, on the largest side of a box grater. Keep grating any larger pieces until you have evenly sized pieces. Alternatively, pulse in a food processor until the mixture resembles breadcrumbs.

Heat a little olive oil in a skillet or frying pan over high heat and fry the grated cauliflower for 3–5 minutes.

In a separate dry skillet or small frying pan, toast the pine nuts over medium heat, until golden.

Add the toasted pine nuts, golden raisins (sultanas), and dried mint to the cauliflower. Stir through the lemon juice, olive oil, shallot, and salt. Taste and adjust seasoning. Serve with a scattering of feta cheese, if desired (in which case you may need to add less salt).

Citrus-Glazed Carrots with Spiced Pistachios

PREPARATION TIME
15 minutes

COOKING TIME
5 minutes

SERVES
4–6 as small plates

1 lb 10 oz/750 g carrots, peeled
juice of ½ orange
juice of ½ lemon
1 tablespoon olive oil
1 teaspoon honey
generous pinch of salt
½ cup (2 oz/50 g) shelled pistachios, coarsely chopped
½ teaspoon Lebanese 7-Spice Seasoning (see page 12)

Carrot and orange is such a natural flavor combination. When the weather is cooler, I love roasting them together to intensify the sweetness of each. But in this summery dish, I keep the ingredients raw with the added crunch of pistachios to make a really easy salad that comes together in minutes, although it tastes as though it has taken much longer to prepare. A vegetable peeler makes quick work of preparing the carrots, or you could carefully use a mandoline to slice thin ribbons or the widest setting on your box grater, if you find that easier.

PREPARATION
Peel the carrots into ribbons using a vegetable peeler or mandoline.

Put the orange and lemon juices, olive oil, honey, and salt in a large bowl and stir to combine. Mix in the carrot ribbons.

Toast the pistachios in a dry skillet or frying pan over medium heat for 3–4 minutes, or until lightly golden around the edges. Stir in the spice seasoning and cook for 30 seconds more, to release the flavor.

Scatter the spiced pistachios over the carrots and serve.

CHAPTER FOUR

Vegetables

Roasted Cauliflower with Tahini and Smoky Paprika

PREPARATION TIME
15 minutes

COOKING TIME
1 hour–1 hour 5 minutes

SERVES
6

FOR THE CAULIFLOWER
1 large cauliflower (about
    2 ¾ lb/1.3 kg), tough outer
    leaves removed
olive oil, for drizzling
salt and pepper

FOR THE TAHINI SAUCE
4 tablespoons Tahini (see
    page 12)
3 tablespoons olive oil
zest and juice of ½ lemon
drizzle of date molasses or
    honey, to taste
salt and pepper

FOR THE PAPRIKA DRESSING
4 tablespoons extra virgin
    olive oil
3 garlic cloves, finely sliced
1 red chile, finely chopped
1 teaspoon dried oregano
1 teaspoon hot smoked paprika
juice of ½ lemon
1 small bunch parsley, leaves
    only, coarsely chopped

A cauliflower, roasted whole, charred, and caramelized at the edges, is one of the most glorious ways to add a delicious centerpiece to any mezze spread, in my opinion. I like to serve it with a sharp knife so everyone can dig in and help themselves.

PREPARATION
Preheat the oven to 375°F/190°C/Gas Mark 5.

Generously drizzle the cauliflower with olive oil, then put it into a small roasting pan. Pour 5 tablespoons of water into the bottom of the pan, taking care not to splash the cauliflower with water as you do, otherwise it may become soggy in the oven. Cover the tray with aluminum foil and roast in the oven for 40 minutes.

Meanwhile, make the tahini sauce. Add all the ingredients to a mixing bowl and mix well to combine. Taste and adjust the seasoning. Whisk the sauce while slowly pouring in 3 tablespoons of cold water (you may need a helper to hold the bowl for you). The sauce should turn a shade lighter and have the consistency of Greek yogurt. Check the seasoning again, and set aside.

Remove the cauliflower from the oven and turn the temperature up to 425°F/220°C/Gas Mark 7. Lift the foil from the pan, and season the cauliflower generously with salt and pepper. Return to the oven for a further 20–25 minutes, until the cauliflower is crispy, deep golden, and starting to blacken in places.

Meanwhile, make the paprika dressing. Warm the olive oil for the dressing in a small skillet or frying pan over medium heat. Add the garlic and chile, and fry for 2 minutes until fragrant and the garlic is starting to take on a little color. Add the dried oregano and smoked paprika to the pan and cook for a further 30 seconds. Remove from the heat, stir in the lemon juice and set aside.

Spread the tahini sauce on a serving platter and put the cauliflower in the center. Pour over the smoky paprika dressing to impart as much flavor as possible to all of the cauliflower's crevices. Sprinkle over the parsley and serve immediately.

Onions Roasted with Orange and Thyme

PREPARATION TIME
10 minutes

COOKING TIME
1 hour 30 minutes

SERVES
6–8

7 tablespoons (3 ½ oz/100 g) unsalted butter
1 small bunch thyme
1 tablespoon balsamic vinegar
1 tablespoon pomegranate molasses
juice of 1 orange
5 onions, peeled
salt and pepper

This dish elevates the onion from a foundation flavor to a dish in its own right. Cooked slowly and with care, they are buttery, caramelized, and delicious. This would also work well with fennel and little pieces of Preserved Lemon (see page 26) with the onions, just swap the balsamic vinegar for apple cider vinegar instead.

PREPARATION
Preheat the oven to 400°F/200°C/Gas Mark 6.

Melt the butter in a small skillet or frying pan over high heat. When it is foaming, add the thyme, balsamic vinegar, pomegranate molasses, and orange juice. Reduce the heat to medium and cook for 2 minutes, until everything is fragrant and looks emulsified.

Trim each end of the onions, so they will sit flat on top and bottom. Halve them around the middle and place the halves, middle facing up, in a smallish roasting pan so that they're tightly packed. Pour the melted butter mixture over the top of the onions and season generously with salt and pepper.

Cover the tray with aluminum foil and roast in the hot oven for 45 minutes, then remove the foil and return the tray to the oven for a further 45 minutes, basting three or four times with the flavored butter at the bottom of the pan.

Serve warm as part of a mezze spread.

Shredded Brussels Sprouts with Walnuts

PREPARATION TIME
15 minutes

COOKING TIME
10 minutes

SERVES
4 as small plates

1 lb 2 oz/500 g Brussels sprouts, washed, outer leaves removed
⅓ cup (2 oz/50 g) walnut halves
½ teaspoon cumin seeds
1 tablespoon olive oil
pinch of salt
1 tablespoon pomegranate molasses
toasted flatbread, to serve
thick Greek yogurt, to serve
Za'atar (see page 13), to serve
olive oil, to serve

Brussels sprouts are such a divisive vegetable, but treated with care (and admittedly with some other complementary ingredients), they are worth celebrating well before and beyond Christmas. I like them cooked in a really hot pan, and browned in places, which seems to work well with so many members of the brassica family.

This recipe would also work well with spring greens or green cabbage in place of the Brussels sprouts.

PREPARATION

Trim the base from the sprouts and discard. Lay each sprout flat on the cut bottom and shred finely with a very sharp knife.

Toast the walnut halves in a dry skillet or frying pan over low heat for 6–8 minutes, shaking the pan frequently, until golden and toasted. Add the cumin seeds and cook for 30 seconds, until fragrant. Transfer the walnuts and cumin seeds to a small bowl and set aside.

Add the olive oil to the same pan, turn the heat up to medium-high, and add the Brussels sprouts and salt. Cook, stirring continuously, for 5 minutes, until the sprouts are starting to catch in places and have started to reduce (they should still be a verdant green color). Stir in the pomegranate molasses, walnuts, and cumin, then cook for a further 30 seconds, tossing the pan a couple of times until everything is incorporated.

Serve warm with some toasted flatbread and yogurt topped with za'atar and oil, or stuffed into a falafel wrap.

Za'atar Mushrooms with Buckwheat Pancakes

PREPARATION TIME
10 minutes + 2 hours resting

COOKING TIME
35 minutes

SERVES
6–8 pancakes

FOR THE PANCAKES
¾ cup (3 ½ oz/100 g) wholemeal buckwheat flour
1 egg
scant ½ cup (3 ½ fl oz/100 ml) almond milk
pinch of salt and pepper
freshly grated nutmeg
few sprigs of thyme, leaves only
olive oil, for frying

FOR THE FILLING
olive oil, for frying
3 ½ oz/100 g spinach
1 lb 2 oz/500 g chestnut mushrooms, wiped and quartered
2 garlic cloves, finely chopped
1 tablespoon Za'atar (see page 13)
3 ½ oz/100 g feta cheese, crumbled
salt and pepper

This is a lovely, filling, and interesting combination of flavors. I'm sure it would also work well as a brunch dish with poached eggs, if you're trying to impress your guests.

PREPARATION

Start by making the pancakes; in a small pitcher (jug), whisk together the flour, egg, and almond milk until the mixture is completely smooth. Add a generous pinch each of salt, pepper, nutmeg, and the thyme leaves. Stir to combine, then cover and rest in the refrigerator for 2 hours.

When the resting time for the pancake batter is up, heat a drizzle of olive oil in a large skillet or frying pan over medium heat. Add the spinach, stirring regularly with a wooden spoon until the leaves are deep green and wilted, then put them into a strainer (sieve), pushing down with the back of a wooden spoon to remove as much moisture as possible. Set aside.

Wipe the pan dry with paper towels, then dry-fry the mushrooms with a pinch of salt over medium heat for 8 minutes, stirring regularly. The mushrooms will steam, then begin to release water and reduce in size. As soon as most of the water is cooked off and the mushrooms have started to take on a little color, add another splash of oil, and the garlic. Stir-fry for 1 minute, then stir in the za'atar and wilted spinach. Taste and adjust the seasoning with salt and pepper. Crumble over the feta cheese in large chunks, then set aside in the pan until ready to serve.

Remove the pancake batter from the refrigerator and heat enough olive oil to coat the bottom of a skillet or frying pan over medium-high heat. When the oil is almost smoking, pour about a sixth of the batter into the pan, tilting and swirling the pan immediately so that the batter coats the bottom of the pan. Cook for a couple of minutes until the pancake turns a lighter color and starts to lift at the edges, then use a spatula to flip it over and cook the other side. I always find the first pancake is the trickiest, but you'll get the hang of it. Keep warm, stacked between wax (greaseproof) paper, while you cook the remaining pancakes, adding a little more oil to the pan if you need to.

While you are cooking the last pancake, quickly reheat the filling in its pan without stirring.

Serve each pancake with the za'atar mushroom filling piled in the center, and perhaps some vegetable pickles to go alongside.

Shakshuka

PREPARATION TIME	COOKING TIME	SERVES
10 minutes	45 minutes	4

olive oil, for frying
1 red onion, finely chopped
2 sweet pointed (Romano) red peppers, seeded and cut into 1-inch (2-cm) dice
3 garlic cloves, finely chopped
1 small bunch cilantro (coriander), leaves picked and stalks finely sliced
½ teaspoon Lebanese 7-Spice Seasoning (see page 12)
½ teaspoon chili powder
1 tablespoon coriander seeds, coarsely bashed in a pestle and mortar
1 teaspoon hot smoked paprika
7 oz/200 g mixed cherry tomatoes, halved
1 (14-oz/400-g) can chopped tomatoes
1 teaspoon superfine (caster) sugar
4 eggs
4 teaspoons thick Greek yogurt
salt and pepper
toasted flatbreads, to serve

This is what I think of when I want to conjure up a Middle Eastern breakfast. It's a one-pan dish, so it's easy to prepare, hearty, and rich; just as home on the mezze table as it is at the beginning of the day. If I have roasted peppers around, I'll often coarsely chop them and stir them in with the tomatoes.

PREPARATION
Heat a generous splash of olive oil in a skillet or frying pan over medium heat. Add the onion and a pinch of salt and cook for 8–10 minutes, until soft and sweet. Stir in the peppers, garlic, and chopped cilantro (coriander) stalks and cook for a further 5 minutes, until the pepper is starting to soften and take on some color. Push the peppers and onion to the side of the pan, then add the spices to the exposed pan. Toast for 1 minute, then stir through the pepper and onion. Add the cherry tomatoes and stir to combine. Cook for another 5 minutes, until you feel the tomatoes begin to soften. Add the chopped tomatoes and sugar, and turn the heat down to medium–low. Simmer for 15 minutes, to let the flavors develop and the sauce thicken.

Make four little wells in the mixture and crack in the eggs. Turn the heat up to medium–high and cook the eggs for 6–8 minutes until the whites are set. If necessary, cover the pan with a lid to cook the eggs through.

Dot the yogurt around the pan and scatter over the cilantro (coriander) leaves. Serve with toasted flatbreads at the center of your mezze table.

Orange Blossom Labneh with Squash

PREPARATION TIME
10 minutes + 6 hours straining

COOKING TIME
40 minutes + 10 minutes cooling

SERVES
4 as small plates

FOR THE ORANGE BLOSSOM LABNEH
scant 1 cup (7 oz/200 g) thick Greek yogurt
1 teaspoon orange blossom water
1 teaspoon date syrup
zest of ½ orange
pinch of flaky sea salt

FOR THE SQUASH
1 lb 2 oz/500 g squash, peeled and chopped into ¾-inch/2-cm pieces
olive oil for drizzling
½ teaspoon cumin seeds
½ cup (2 oz/50 g) shelled pistachios
salt and pepper

Once you have made traditional (unflavored) labneh once or twice, you will have the confidence to experiment with different flavorings, from herbs to citrus zests. I like this slightly sweetened version, which pairs beautifully with squash or beets (beetroot).

If you are short on time, you could substitute fresh curd cheese for the Greek yogurt, which will remove the need for straining time.

PREPARATION
First, make the labneh. Mix all the ingredients together in a bowl and taste to check that you're happy with the flavor (the aromatic flavors will remain after the yogurt has thickened). Line a strainer (sieve) with a double thickness of cheesecloth (muslin) and set over a large bowl. Use a rubber spatula to scrape the yogurt mixture into the center of the cloth, then fold the sides of the cloth over the top to completely cover the yogurt. Place in the refrigerator for at least 6 hours until thickened and all the liquid has drained off. Check occasionally to make sure the bottom of the strainer is not touching the liquid. If it is, pour away the liquid.

Preheat the oven to 400°F/200°C/Gas Mark 6.

Toss the squash in a bowl with the olive oil, cumin seeds, and some salt and pepper. Arrange the squash in a single layer (without overlapping) on a baking sheet, then roast in the oven for about 40 minutes, until completely soft and browning at the edges.

Spread the pistachios over a separate baking sheet and place in the oven for the final 5 minutes of the squash cooking time.

Remove both baking sheets from the oven, setting the squash aside to cool on the sheet. Transfer the pistachios to a chopping board to cool.

When the pistachios are cool enough to handle, coarsely chop or bash them in a pestle and mortar.

Ripple the labneh over a large serving plate. When the squash has cooled to lukewarm, arrange it over the orange blossom-scented labneh, then scatter over the pistachios. Serve immediately.

Roasted Turnips with Sumac and Fresh Thyme

PREPARATION TIME
5 minutes

COOKING TIME
30–35 minutes

SERVES
2–3 as small plates

1 lb 2 oz/500 g turnips, quartered, or swede, cut into irregular 1¼-inch (3-cm) chunks
olive oil, for drizzling
1 tablespoon sumac
zest of 1 orange and juice of ½
few sprigs of thyme
salt and pepper

Turnips are seriously underappreciated, but are a popular vegetable in the Middle East where we make the most of their intriguing radish-like flavor by preparing them in a myriad of interesting ways. Here, I roast turnips with the dried sumac berry, which adds a lovely citrus brightness that pairs so well with the fiery flavor of this inexpensive and nutritious root.

You could also make this dish with swede, which is similar in flavor but slightly sweeter, with less heat. Any leftovers make a great addition thrown in with a lunchbox salad.

PREPARATION
Preheat the oven to 375°F/190°C/Gas Mark 5.

Toss the prepared vegetables in a small roasting pan with enough olive oil to coat and the sumac. Squeeze the orange juice over and toss to combine.

Roast in the center of the oven for 35 minutes, then remove the roasting pan and nestle the thyme sprigs among the vegetables. Return to the oven for 5–10 minutes, until the vegetables are tender and starting to wrinkle at the sides.

Season with the orange zest, salt, and pepper before serving.

Sweet Potatoes with Tahini and Pul Biber

PREPARATION TIME
5 minutes

COOKING TIME
25 minutes

SERVES
4-6

2 large sweet potatoes (about 1 lb 5 oz/600 g), peeled and cut into wedges
olive oil, for drizzling
1 tablespoon pul biber (Turkish chili flakes)
salt and pepper

FOR THE TAHINI SAUCE
4½ tablespoons Tahini (see page 12)
zest and juice of 1 lemon
2 small garlic cloves, finely chopped
drizzle of date molasses or honey, to taste
generous pinch of Za'atar (see page 13)
salt and pepper

I haven't always been the biggest fan of sweet potatoes, but recently I've been experimenting with different flavors and ways of cooking them (see my Harissa Sweet Potato Cakes on page 128); they work really well with Middle Eastern and Asian flavors such as tahini and yogurt, or peanut and lime. This somewhat echoes my philosophy on cooking: being open to new techniques and ideas, and not afraid of change and progress.

PREPARATION
Preheat the oven to 425°F/220°C/Gas Mark 7.
  Toss the sweet potato wedges with a drizzle of olive oil and the pul biber.
  Roast in the hot oven for 25 minutes, turning once during the cooking time.
  Meanwhile, mix all the ingredients for the tahini sauce, apart from the za'atar, in a mixing bowl. Using a balloon whisk and stirring all the time, pour 4–6 tablespoons of cold water in a slow stream into the tahini mixture, until the sauce turns a couple of shades lighter and looks airier and fluffy. Taste and adjust the seasoning, then spoon into a small serving bowl and sprinkle the za'atar over the top.
  Remove the sweet potatoes from the oven and season with salt and pepper while still warm. Serve alongside the tahini dressing as part of a mezze spread.

Celery Root with Toasted Spices

PREPARATION TIME
20 minutes

COOKING TIME
45 minutes

SERVES
6 as small plates

1 celery root (celeriac)
1 tablespoon butter, plus extra as needed
1 teaspoon smoked paprika
1 teaspoon ground cinnamon
1 teaspoon coriander seeds, crushed in a pestle and mortar
1 lemon, halved
salt and pepper

I've found that celery root (celeriac) is an unpopular vegetable, with its tough, knobbly skin and alien appearance, but I love its flavor; sort of like a celery crossed with a potato, making it a perfect complementary vehicle for a host of interesting flavors.

PREPARATION

Preheat the oven to 375°F/190°C/Gas Mark 5. Line a baking sheet with parchment (baking) paper.

Peel the celery root (celeriac) with a large, sharp knife and, resting the bottom flat edge on the chopping board, cut it into ¾-inch/2-cm thick slices. Cut each slice into irregular pieces (about 10 little chunks from each slice).

Add the butter to a large skillet or frying pan and cook over medium heat until it starts to sizzle and turn a nutty color. Fry the celery root in batches, taking care not to overcrowd the pan, for 6-8 minutes, turning occasionally, until golden brown in places. Keep an eye on the heat and the butter—you may need to turn the heat down if the butter is smoking a lot, or add more butter to the pan as the celery root will absorb it as it cooks.

Arrange the cooked celery root pieces in a single layer (without overlapping) on the prepared baking sheet, and sprinkle over the spices. Toss to combine, then nestle the lemon halves in among the pieces. Bake in the oven for 20 minutes until the celery root is cooked through.

Before serving, use tongs to carefully squeeze the lemon halves over the celery root (they will be hot!). Season with salt and pepper and serve while still hot.

Classic Batata Harra

PREPARATION TIME
15 minutes + 30 minutes soaking time

COOKING TIME
15 minutes

SERVES
4 as small plates

1 lb 2 oz/500 g firm-fleshed potatoes (such as Desiree), peeled and cut into ¾-inch/1.5-cm cubes
1 teaspoon cumin seeds
¼ teaspoon ground turmeric
pinch of chili powder (optional)
4–5 tablespoons vegetable oil
1 small bunch cilantro (coriander), chopped
salt and pepper

See pages 108–109 for image

I soak the potatoes here to remove some of the starch and prevent them from sticking in the pan.

This is my version of crispy roasted potatoes. Because potatoes generally have quite a neutral flavor, they adopt stronger flavors well. I like to experiment with spices and other seasonings like lemon and herbs.

PREPARATION
Place the potatoes in a large bowl, cover with cold water and set aside for 30 minutes, then drain and dry well on paper towels.

Toast the cumin seeds in a small, dry skillet or frying pan over low heat for a few minutes, shaking the pan occasionally, until aromatic. Remove from the heat, transfer to a pestle and mortar and grind coarsely. Tip them into a large bowl, stir in the turmeric and chili powder (if using), and season with salt and pepper. Add the potatoes to the bowl and toss to coat in the spices.

Add the oil (to a depth of about ¼ inch/5 mm) to a skillet or frying pan set over medium heat. When hot, add the potatoes and cook for 10–15 minutes, tossing the pan frequently, until they are golden and crisp with a tender center. Remove with a slotted spoon to drain on paper towels.

Season, then serve warm, with the chopped cilantro (coriander) stirred through.

Fried Potatoes with Lebanese 7-Spice Sauce

PREPARATION TIME
15 minutes + 30 minutes soaking time

COOKING TIME
1 hour 10 minutes

SERVES
4 as small plates

FOR THE POTATOES
1 lb 2 oz/500 g firm-fleshed potatoes (such as Desiree), peeled and cut into ¾-inch/1.5-cm cubes
4–5 tablespoons vegetable oil
salt and pepper

FOR THE SAUCE
1 small onion, finely chopped
olive oil, for frying
2 garlic cloves, finely sliced
1 red chile, finely sliced, with seeds
1 teaspoon Lebanese 7-Spice Seasoning (see page 12)
1 lb 8 ½ oz/700 g mixed tomatoes, coarsely chopped
1 bay leaf
sea salt

See pages 108–109 for image

A sort of Middle Eastern twist on the Spanish favorite, patatas bravas (fried potatoes with spicy tomato sauce). I use my special Lebanese 7 Spice Seasoning to add a distinct Middle Eastern flavor to the sauce.

PREPARATION
Place the potatoes in a large bowl, cover with cold water and set aside for 30 minutes, then drain and dry on paper towels.

Meanwhile, make the sauce. Heat a splash of olive oil in a large saucepan over medium heat. Add the onion and cook for 8–10 minutes, until soft, sweet, and translucent, but not taking on any color. Stir in the garlic and chile, and cook for 1 minute. Stir in the spice seasoning, and cook for 30 seconds to release the oils. Add the tomatoes and bay leaf and bring to a simmer, then reduce the heat to low and cook for 45 minutes, until the sauce has reduced by a third and the tomatoes have completely broken down. Check seasoning and set aside.

Add the oil (to a depth of about ¼ inch/5 mm) to a skillet or frying pan set over medium heat. When hot, add the potatoes and cook for 10–15 minutes, tossing the pan frequently, until they are golden and crisp with a tender center. Remove with a slotted spoon to drain on paper towels.

Season, then serve the potatoes warm, with the sauce poured over.

1. Fried Potatoes with Lebanese 7-Spice Sauce (p. 107)

2. Classic Batata Harra (p.106) 3. Fried Potatoes with Fennel and Green Olives (p.111) 4. Fried Potatoes with Preserved Lemon and Mint (p. 110)

Fried Potatoes with Preserved Lemon and Mint

PREPARATION TIME
15 minutes + 30 minutes soaking time

COOKING TIME
15 minutes

SERVES
4 as small plates

1 lb 2 oz/500 g firm-fleshed potatoes (such as Desiree), peeled and cut into ¾-inch/1.5-cm cubes
4–5 tablespoons vegetable oil
2 thumb-sized pieces Preserved Lemon (see page 26), flesh discarded and rind finely chopped
1 small bunch mint, leaves only
juice of ½ lemon
salt and pepper

See pages 108–109 for image

Lemons and potatoes are such a great flavor combination; I implore you to add a halved lemon to the roasting tray when you're cooking your potatoes for a family get together. Preserved lemons work just as well, and I've added mint to bring a fresh note to this dish.

PREPARATION

Place the potatoes in a large bowl, cover with cold water and set aside for 30 minutes, then drain and dry on paper towels.

Add the oil (to a depth of about ¼ inch/5 mm) to a skillet or frying pan set over medium heat. When hot, add the potatoes and cook for 10–15 minutes, tossing the pan frequently, until they are golden and crisp with a tender center. Remove with a slotted spoon to drain on paper towels.

Toss the preserved lemon and mint leaves through the fried potatoes, season, then finish with lemon juice, to taste.

Fried Potatoes with Fennel and Green Olives

PREPARATION TIME
15 minutes + 30 minutes soaking time

COOKING TIME
15 minutes

SERVES
4 as small plates

- 1 lb 2 oz/500 g firm-fleshed potatoes (such as Desiree), peeled and cut into ¾-inch/1.5-cm cubes
- 4–5 tablespoons vegetable oil
- 1 fennel bulb, finely sliced, fronds reserved
- 3 ½ oz/100 g pitted green olives, coarsely chopped
- zest of 1 lemon
- salt and pepper

See pages 108–109 for image

This is a delicious addition to a mezze spread, and would work particularly well alongside chicken or fish.

PREPARATION

Place the potatoes in a large bowl, cover with cold water and set aside for 30 minutes, then drain and dry on kitchen paper.

Add the oil (to a depth of about ¼ inch/5 mm) to a skillet or frying pan set over medium heat. When hot, add the potatoes and cook for about 10 minutes, tossing the pan frequently. Just before the potatoes are done (when they've started to take on some color, but are not yet golden brown), add the sliced fennel and cook for 5 minutes, stirring regularly, until the fennel has softened and is starting to crisp at the edges, and the potatoes are golden and crisp with a tender center. Remove the potato and fennel with a slotted spoon to drain on paper towels.

Transfer to a serving bowl, sprinkle with salt, add a crack of black pepper, and toss through the green olives and lemon zest. Serve topped with the reserved fennel fronds.

Crispy Eggplant with Grape Molasses

PREPARATION TIME
10 minutes + 45 minutes soaking

COOKING TIME
20–25 minutes

SERVES
4 as small plates

1 large eggplant (aubergine), cut into ½-inch (1-cm) lengths, then into chunky chip-sized pieces
generous 2 cups (17 fl oz/ 500 ml) whole milk or nut milk
½ cup (3 oz/80 g) fine-ground polenta
¾ cup (3 oz/80 g) cornstarch (cornflour)
salt and pepper
vegetable or sunflower oil, for frying
¼ cup (2 fl oz/50 ml) grape molasses or pomegranate molasses

I first tried eggplant (aubergines) like this at Morito, one of my favorite tapas bars in London. They serve their dish with whipped feta and date molasses, a flavor combination that works so well together. I find that these crispy eggplant fries work just as well without the cheese as part of a mezze spread.

PREPARATION

Place the eggplant (aubergine) in a bowl with the milk and use a small plate to weigh it down, so that the eggplant is covered with the milk. Set aside to soak for at least 45 minutes.

Drain the eggplant, discarding the bitter liquid, and pat dry with paper towels.

In a large bowl, mix the polenta, cornstarch (cornflour), and some salt and pepper, until evenly combined. Toss the eggplant through until every piece is covered.

Heat 4 tablespoons of oil in a large skillet or frying pan over medium heat. Working in 3 or 4 batches, fry the eggplant in the hot oil, until the pieces are golden all over, adding more oil when the pan is looking dry. Lift out the crispy fried eggplant with a slotted spoon and drain on paper towels.

Drizzle the molasses over while still warm and serve immediately with some paper napkins.

Roasted Squash with Middle Eastern Spices

PREPARATION TIME
10 minutes

COOKING TIME
40 minutes

SERVES
4-6 (depending on the size of the squash)

- 1 ¾ lb/800 g butternut or other squash (I like crown prince and delicata squash), peeled, seeded, and chopped into 1-inch (2-cm) pieces
- olive oil, for drizzling
- ½ teaspoon cumin seeds
- ½ teaspoon coriander seeds, coarsely bashed in a pestle and mortar
- ½ teaspoon ground cinnamon
- ½ teaspoon ground turmeric
- salt and pepper
- Za'atar (see page 13), to serve (optional)

I'm sure this would be delicious with za'atar sprinkled over the top, but I've exercised restraint in this recipe to let the individual flavors of the spices shine through. Do try it though, if you have za'atar to hand! Serve as part of a mezze selection.

PREPARATION
Preheat the oven to 425°F/220°C/Gas Mark 7.

In a large mixing bowl, mix the squash with a generous drizzle of olive oil, the spices, and some salt and pepper, tossing to coat.

Arrange the squash in a single layer (without overlapping) over a roasting pan lined with parchment (baking) paper, then roast in the oven for 35–40 minutes, until soft right through and browning at the edges.

Sprinkle with za'atar before serving, if desired.

Grilled Purple Sprouting Broccoli and Halloumi

PREPARATION TIME
5 minutes

COOKING TIME
20 minutes

SERVES
4 as small plates

9 oz/250 g purple sprouting broccoli, tough ends trimmed
2 tablespoons sesame seeds
2 tablespoons extra virgin olive oil
½ Preserved Lemon (see page 26), flesh discarded and rind finely chopped
3 ½ oz/100 g halloumi, cut into ½-inch (1-cm) slices
salt

See pages 118–119 for image

If the purple sprouting broccoli is really leafy, with larger leaves than heads, remove the leaves before boiling and blanch separately for a minute. Grill the leaves after the broccoli heads to ensure everything is ready at the same time.

PREPARATION
Heat a ridged grill (griddle) pan over the highest heat.

Fill a large saucepan with boiling water and salt generously. Bring to a rolling boil, then plunge the broccoli in and boil fast for 2–3 minutes, depending on the thickness of the stalks. Drain in a colander under very cold running water for at least 1 minute to stop the cooking process.

Toast the sesame seeds in a small dry skillet or frying pan over medium heat for about 4 minutes, stirring frequently, until the sesame seeds are golden. Remove from the heat and let cool for 30 seconds, before stirring in the oil and finely chopped lemon rind.

Shake as much water as you can from the purple sprouting broccoli, then cook on the hot grill pan for 2–3 minutes each side, until charred but still bright green. When the broccoli is cooked through, place on a platter and keep warm in the oven.

Grill the halloumi for 1 minute on each side, until soft and golden.

Arrange the halloumi over the broccoli on the platter, then drizzle over the lemon and sesame dressing.

Cabbage and Apple Slaw

PREPARATION TIME
10 minutes + 30 minutes standing time

COOKING TIME
–

SERVES
4–6 as small plates

FOR THE SLAW
½ white cabbage (about 14 oz/ 400 g), cored and finely shredded
2 tart eating apples (such as Braeburn), cored, sliced, and chopped into small triangles
juice of 1 lemon
pinch of salt
1 small bunch parsley, finely chopped (remove any tough stalks)

FOR THE DRESSING
2 tablespoons Tahini (see page 12)
3 tablespoons olive oil
1 garlic clove, crushed
juice of ½ lemon, or to taste
1 teaspoon date syrup, or to taste
½ teaspoon salt, or to taste

See page 79 for image

This is my Middle Eastern take on a Waldorf salad, and I'm sure the addition of some finely sliced celery and lightly toasted walnuts wouldn't go amiss here.

PREPARATION
Put the cabbage, apple, and lemon juice into a mixing bowl, together with a pinch of salt and mix well. Set aside.

Mix all the dressing ingredients together. Taste and add more lemon juice, date syrup, and salt, according to preference. Loosen with a little water if wished. Toss the dressing through the slaw, then mix through the chopped parsley.

Leave the salad to develop its flavors for 30 minutes before serving.

1. Zucchini Kuku (p.120) 2. Red Cabbage and Pomegranate (p.121) 3. Grilled Purple Sprouting Broccoli and Halloumi (p.116)

Zucchini Kuku

PREPARATION TIME	COOKING TIME	SERVES
10 minutes	25 minutes	4–6

olive oil, for frying
1 red onion, finely chopped
pinch of salt
3 garlic cloves, finely sliced
1 red chile, finely chopped
3 medium zucchini
   (courgettes), finely sliced
4 eggs, beaten
1 small bunch mixed herbs
   (parsley, dill, tarragon)

FOR THE SPICE BLEND
¼ teaspoon ground ginger
¼ teaspoon ground turmeric
¼ teaspoon Lebanese 7-Spice
   Seasoning (see page 12)
¼ teaspoon ground coriander
grating of nutmeg

See pages 118–119 for image

Zucchini (courgette) kuku is really just a Middle Eastern way of saying zucchini frittata. Lightly spiced, this dish packs a punch in terms of flavor and texture and comes together quickly in the pan.

PREPARATION
Mix all of the ingredients for the spice blend and set aside.
   Heat the broiler (grill) to high.
   Heat a splash of olive oil in an ovenproof skillet or frying pan, then add the red onion and salt. Cook over medium heat for 5–8 minutes until soft, sweet, and translucent. Add the garlic, chile, spice blend, and zucchini (courgettes), and continue to cook for 8 minutes, stirring, until the zucchini have reduced by about a third and are softening and catching at the edges. Pour over the eggs and mix in the herbs. Cook for 5 minutes until set on the bottom. Finish under the hot broiler, until the eggs are set on top and the zucchini are charring a little.
   Serve at the center of a mezze selection.

Red Cabbage and Pomegranate

PREPARATION TIME
15 minutes

COOKING TIME
1 hour 30 minutes

SERVES
6–8

1 tablespoon olive oil
1 tablespoon butter
2 red onions, sliced
1 red cabbage, cored and shredded
1 apple, peeled, cored and grated
1 cinnamon stick
½ teaspoon ground allspice
2 tablespoons red wine vinegar
3 tablespoons brown sugar
juice of ½ orange
4 tablespoons pomegranate syrup
⅓ cup (2 oz/50 g) raisins

See pages 118–119 for image

I love the way that the English prepare their red cabbage in the winter; stewed slowly with apples and some spices, it makes a perfect accompaniment to meat and roasted vegetables. In this recipe, I have added a surprising Middle Eastern twist with the pomegranate syrup, which works so well with red cabbage when cooked down slowly like this.

PREPARATION
Put all the ingredients into a heavy-based saucepan set over a low heat. Mix well, then cover and cook, stirring occasionally, for 1 hour and 30 minutes. Serve immediately.

Jerusalem Artichoke and Orange Soup

PREPARATION TIME
15 minutes

COOKING TIME
30 minutes

SERVES
8

generous glug of olive oil
1 large onion, finely chopped
1 lb 8½ oz/700 g Jerusalem artichokes
2 garlic cloves, finely chopped
1 small bunch lemon thyme
4¼ cups (34 fl oz/1 liter) vegetable stock
⅔ cup (5 fl oz/150 ml) vegetable oil
zest and juice of 1 orange
salt and pepper

This is the only soup in this book because I couldn't decide whether a soup had any place in a mezze book. This silky smooth soup is so delicious that the answer had to be a resounding yes. Serve it warm in small bowls or cups that can be sipped.

PREPARATION
Warm the olive oil in a large saucepan over medium heat. Add the onion with a pinch of salt and cook for 8–10 minutes, until soft and translucent.

Meanwhile, prepare the Jerusalem artichokes: peel them, setting two whole ones aside and quartering the rest.

When the onion is soft, add the garlic, artichoke quarters, lemon thyme, and stock and bring to the boil. Turn the heat down to medium-low and simmer for 20 minutes.

While the soup is cooking, finely slice the reserved artichokes with a mandoline or sharp knife into thin rounds.

Heat the vegetable oil in a small saucepan over medium heat. After about 1 minute, test whether the oil is hot enough by adding a cube of bread—it should crisp and brown straight away and be crispy and golden in 30 seconds. When the oil is hot enough, add the sliced artichokes to the oil and fry for 30 seconds on one side. Use a slotted spoon to turn them over to color on the other side, then remove to paper towels to crisp up.

Pour the soup into a blender and add half the orange zest and all the orange juice. Blitz, until completely smooth, then taste to check the seasoning. You could also use an immersion (stick) blender if you don't have a jug blender, but I find that the consistency often isn't as smooth, although the flavor will be delicious nonetheless.

Ladle the soup into bowls, and top with the Jerusalem artichoke crisps and the remaining orange zest.

# CHAPTER FIVE
Stuffed & Fried

Turkish Scrambled Eggs

PREPARATION TIME
5 minutes

COOKING TIME
20 minutes

SERVES
2 as a breakfast
or 4 as small plates

3 tablespoons olive oil
2 shallots, finely chopped
1 green Turkish pepper or
　3 Padrón peppers, finely
　chopped
½ teaspoon hot smoked paprika
½ teaspoon dried oregano or
　marjoram
½ (14-oz/400-g) can chopped
　tomatoes
4 eggs
salt and pepper

TO SERVE
toast or flatbread
2 tablespoons thick Greek
　yogurt (optional)
generous pinch of pul biber
　(Turkish chili flakes)
1 small bunch parsley, chopped

This dish is called Menemen and is one of the tastiest egg dishes around, but just as good with silken tofu if you want a vegan version. I like to use the paler, pointed Turkish green peppers for this recipe, which can be found in a whole host of corner stores, although they seem to be more difficult to track down in the supermarket. If you're struggling, a bell pepper, a small jalapeño pepper, or a few Padrón peppers will do the trick.

PREPARATION
Heat the olive oil in a large cast-iron, heavy skillet or frying pan over medium heat, then add the chopped shallots, pepper, paprika, and dried oregano or marjoram, along with a pinch of salt, and a generous grinding of cracked black pepper. Turn the heat down to medium-low and cook for 8–10 minutes, stirring frequently, until completely soft. Add the chopped tomatoes, stir to combine, then turn the heat back up to medium. Cook for a further 4–5 minutes, until the color has deepened and the mixture has thickened. Remove half of the vegetable mixture to a bowl and set aside.

　In a small bowl, gently mix the eggs with a fork to break the yolks (you still want to see the distinct colors in the egg when the dish is finished). Fold the eggs into the remaining vegetable mixture in the pan and cook over low heat until just set. Put the reserved vegetable mixture back into the pan and stir to combine.

　Serve on slices of toast or with flatbread, topped with a dollop of Greek yogurt if wished, followed by a scattering of pul biber and chopped parsley.

Harissa Sweet Potato Cakes

PREPARATION TIME
10 minutes + cooling

COOKING TIME
45 minutes

SERVES
4 (makes 12 cakes)

2 large sweet potatoes, peeled and cut into 1 ¼-inch (3-cm) chunks
1 green chile, seeded if you prefer it less spicy
1 tablespoon harissa paste
2 large garlic cloves, finely chopped
1 small red onion, finely chopped
scant ⅔ cup (3 oz/80 g) all-purpose (plain) flour
1 egg, beaten
few sprigs of cilantro (coriander), coarsely chopped
2 teaspoons soy sauce
zest and juice of ½ lemon
salt and pepper
3 tablespoons vegetable oil, for frying
1 teaspoon harissa paste, to serve
4–6 tablespoons thick Greek yogurt, to serve

Harissa, the aromatic chili paste from the Middle East, can vary in heat, so add less than you think you need, then taste and adjust according to your tolerance for spice.

PREPARATION

Steam the sweet potatoes in a steamer for 20–25 minutes, until tender, then set aside in a colander to cool and steam-dry for at least 30 minutes.

If you don't have a steamer, place the sweet potatoes in a strainer (sieve) that can rest on a large saucepan with a lid. Fill the pan with water, ensuring the bottom of the strainer sits above the water line and steam with the lid on. Seal any cracks around the lid with aluminum foil and take care when removing.

When the sweet potato has completely cooled, put it into a large mixing bowl and mash with a fork, then stir through the other ingredients.

In a large skillet or frying pan, heat a splash of the oil over medium heat. Fry a small, coin-sized amount of the sweet potato mixture for 2 minutes on each side, until crispy and golden. Remove to paper towels to drain any excess oil, then taste the cooked patty. If you think it needs more seasoning, lemon juice, or herb flavor, then now is the time to add it.

Shape the sweet potato mixture into 12 burger-sized patties.

Heat the remaining oil in the pan over medium heat. Working in batches of no more than 3 at a time, fry the sweet potato cakes for 3–5 minutes on each side, until a golden crust forms. Use a slotted spatula (fish slice) to transfer them to paper towels to drain.

To serve, swirl the harissa through the yogurt, then dollop on top of the sweet potato cakes.

Beet and Chickpea Fritters

PREPARATION TIME	COOKING TIME	SERVES
20 minutes + 20 minutes chilling	17–25 minutes	4 (makes 12 fritters)

14 oz/400 g cooked medium beets (beetroot)
¾ cup (3 ½ oz/100 g) drained chickpeas, coarsely chopped
1 small bunch mint, leaves only, finely chopped
3 eggs, beaten
3 tablespoons all-purpose (plain) flour
6 tablespoons vegetable oil, for frying
salt and pepper
green salad, to serve (optional)
Yogurt and Lemon Zest Dressing (see page 21), to serve (optional)

See pages 132–133 for image

Beets (beetroot) are an underrated root; they have a myriad of health benefits, from lowering blood pressure, to aiding digestion. Like any root vegetable though, they usually need a bit of help. I like to make these fritters, with chickpeas for extra protein all year round. You may want to wear gloves when grating the beets as they can stain bright pink.

PREPARATION

Grate the cooked beets (beetroot) on a box grater and drain in a strainer (sieve), pushing out as much liquid as you can. Spread the grated beets out on paper towels to dry.

In a mixing bowl, combine the grated beets, chickpeas, mint, beaten egg, and flour, and season with salt and pepper. Cover with plastic wrap (clingfilm) and refrigerate for 20 minutes before you start cooking.

Heat the oil in a large skillet or frying pan over medium-high heat. After about 1 minute, test whether the oil is hot enough by adding a teaspoon of the batter—it should crisp and bubble at the sides quite quickly. When the oil is hot enough, place dessertspoonfuls of the fritter batter (about half the size of your palm) in the hot oil, flattening them gently with the back of the spoon. Fry no more than 3 fritters at a time as overcrowding the pan will cause them to cook slowly and fall apart. Fry each fritter for 2–3 minutes on each side, until crisp and golden, then carefully transfer to paper towels to drain.

Serve with a green salad and some Yogurt and Lemon Zest Dressing (see page 21), if you like.

Carrot and Pistachio Fritters

PREPARATION TIME
20 minutes

COOKING TIME
50–60 minutes

SERVES
4 (makes 12 fritters)

1 lb 2 oz/500 g carrots, cut into ¾ inch/2 cm rounds
grated zest and juice of 1 orange
1 teaspoon Lebanese 7-Spice Seasoning (see page 12)
1 teaspoon cumin seeds
1 teaspoon coriander seeds, lightly crushed
4 shallots, finely chopped
½ cup (2 oz/50 g) pistachio kernels, coarsely chopped
3 eggs, beaten
3 tablespoons all-purpose (plain) flour
1 small bunch parsley, leaves only, coarsely chopped
4 tablespoons vegetable or light olive oil, for frying
salt and pepper
green salad, to serve

See pages 132–133 for image

I use a little of my Lebanese 7-Spice Seasoning in these fritters, which adds such an interesting and hard to pin down flavor. They're crunchy and light, and are sure to disappear quickly!

Full of lovely, fragrant spice and orange flavors; the carrot brings sweetness, and the nuts add crunch.

PREPARATION

Toss the carrots in a roasting pan with the orange zest, juice, spices, and a pinch of salt. Cover tightly with aluminum foil and bake for 25–35 minutes, checking after 15 minutes to see whether the liquid has evaporated. If the pan is completely dry, add a splash of water, re-cover, and continue cooking.

Meanwhile, heat a splash of oil in a skillet or frying pan over medium heat and fry the shallots, with a pinch of salt, for 4–5 minutes, until soft and translucent. Set aside to cool.

The carrots should now be completely soft when pierced with a knife. Remove the foil from the roasting pan and allow them to steam dry.

After a few minutes, place the carrots in a large mixing bowl and roughly mash with a fork or potato masher. Add the shallots, remaining ingredients, a pinch of salt and pepper, and mix well to combine.

Fill a small bowl with water and wet your fingertips before shaping the fritters into rounds, about 3 inches/8 cm in diameter and ¾ inch/1½ cm thick.

Heat the oil in a large skillet or frying pan over medium-high heat. After about 1 minute, test whether the oil is hot enough by adding a teaspoon of the batter—it should crisp and bubble at the sides quite quickly. When the oil is hot enough, fry the carrot fritters for 3 minutes on each side. Use a slotted spatula (fish slice) to carefully turn the fritters, but do not turn before this time, otherwise the fritters will fall apart. Transfer to paper towels to drain.

Serve with a green salad.

1. Potato, Cauliflower, and Turmeric Fritters (p.135) 2. Carrot and Pistachio Fritters (p.131) 3. Zucchini and Mint Fritters (p.134) 4. Beet and Chickpea Fritters (p.130)

Zucchini and Mint Fritters

PREPARATION TIME
15 minutes + 45 minutes draining

COOKING TIME
40 minutes

SERVES
4 (makes 16 fritters)

- 3 medium zucchini (courgettes) about 1 lb 2 oz/500 g, coarsely grated
- 1 tablespoon olive oil
- 1 onion, finely chopped
- 2 oz/50 g feta cheese
- 1 small bunch mint, coarsely chopped
- 1 small bunch dill, coarsely chopped
- 1 small bunch parsley, coarsely chopped
- 3 tablespoons all-purpose (plain) flour
- 3 eggs, beaten
- 4 tablespoons vegetable oil
- sea salt
- zest and juice of 2 lemons, to serve

See pages 132–133 for image

Zucchini (courgette) fritters are a great thing to make with children; little hands make light work of the grating and shaping. Bound with the herbs, they're fresh and very moreish.

PREPARATION

Toss the grated zucchini (courgettes) with 1 heaping teaspoon of salt and put into a strainer (sieve) set over a bowl for at least 45 minutes to drain.

Meanwhile, heat the olive oil in a skillet or frying pan over medium heat. Add the onion and a pinch of salt, and cook for 10 minutes until soft and sweet. Set aside.

Squeeze out any excess moisture from the zucchini and put onto paper towels to drain briefly.

In a large mixing bowl, combine the zucchini and onion, crumble in the feta cheese, then fold in the chopped herbs, flour, and eggs.

Heat the vegetable oil in a skillet or frying pan over medium heat. After about 1 minute, test whether the oil is hot enough by adding a cube of bread—it should crisp and brown straight away and be crispy and golden in 30 seconds. When the oil is hot enough, working in batches of no more than 4–5 fritters at a time, fry spoonfuls of the fritter mixture for 3 minutes on each side until crispy and golden. Use a slotted spatula (fish slice) to transfer the fritters to paper towels to drain.

Serve with the zest and lemon juice sprinkled over.

Potato, Cauliflower, and Turmeric Fritters

PREPARATION TIME
15 minutes

COOKING TIME
20 minutes

SERVES
4 (makes 8–10 fritters)

3 medium potatoes (about 14 oz/400 g), washed but unpeeled
½ head very fresh cauliflower, broken into tiny ½-inch (1-cm) florets
1 teaspoon ground turmeric or finely grated fresh turmeric
1 small bunch dill, leaves only
4 scallions (spring onions), thinly sliced
4 tablespoons vegetable oil or light olive oil
salt and pepper
Yogurt and Lemon Zest Dressing (see page 21), to serve (optional)

See pages 132–133 for image

The potato acts both as ingredient and binding agent in this recipe, which makes these fritters vegan. I love the English condiment piccalilli and this is my milder version of that in fritter form.

PREPARATION

Put the potatoes into a saucepan of cold water, bring to the boil and cook for 25–30 minutes over medium-high heat, until tender. Drain and set aside in a colander to cool and steam-dry.

When the potatoes are cool enough to handle, rub off their skins and put into a large mixing bowl. Mash them with a potato masher or fork until smooth, then use your hands to squeeze in the cauliflower florets, turmeric, dill, scallions (spring onions), and some salt and pepper, until well mixed.

With wet hands, take golf-ball sized pieces of the potato mixture and mold into small burger shapes with your hands. Repeat to form 8–10 fritters.

Heat half the vegetable oil in a skillet or frying pan over medium heat. After about 1 minute, test whether the oil is hot enough by adding a cube of bread—it should crisp and brown straight away and be crispy and golden in 30 seconds. When the oil is hot enough, working in batches of no more than 4–5 fritters at a time, fry the fritters for 3 minutes on each side until crisp and deep golden. Use a slotted spatula (fish slice) to transfer the fritters to paper towels to drain.

Continue with the remaining fritters, adding more oil to the pan if you need to.

Serve with a green salad and some Yogurt and Lemon Zest Dressing (see page 21), if wished.

Stuffed Peppers with Quinoa

PREPARATION TIME
45 minutes

COOKING TIME
45 minutes

SERVES
6–8 as small plates

3 sweet pointed (Romano) red peppers or red bell peppers, halved lengthwise and seeded
olive oil, for drizzling and frying
⅔ cup (3 ½ oz/100 g) quinoa, rinsed
2 red onions, finely chopped
1 head fennel, finely chopped
1 red chile, finely chopped
1 tablespoon cumin seeds
1 tablespoon pul biber (Turkish chili flakes)
1 teaspoon Lebanese 7-Spice Seasoning (see page 12)
1 (14-oz/400-g) can chopped tomatoes
1 small bunch thyme, leaves only
1 head spring greens, shredded
7 oz/200 g feta cheese
salt and pepper

Filled sweet pointed (Romano) red peppers make a lovely centerpiece in any mezze spread because of their elegant long shape. Sweeter than your average red bell pepper and with a thinner skin, I always buy them when I can. If they're not available though, a normal bell pepper will still do the job nicely. If you have vegetables that need using up, use them here. Try adding grated carrot, or substituting any leafy green vegetable in place of the spring greens.

PREPARATION

Preheat the oven to 350°F/180°C/Gas Mark 4.

Put the pepper halves into a roasting pan, drizzle with olive oil, season with salt and pepper, and roast in the hot oven for 10 minutes.

Meanwhile, cook the quinoa according to the packet directions and drain. Put into a large bowl and set aside.

While the quinoa and peppers are cooking, warm a glug of olive oil in a large skillet or frying pan over medium heat. Add the onions, fennel, and a pinch of salt, and fry for 10 minutes until soft, sweet, and translucent.

Remove the peppers from the oven and set four halves aside (you can leave them in the roasting pan). Chop the remaining two halves into ½-inch (1-cm) pieces and put into the bowl with the quinoa.

Turn the oven up to 400°F/200°C/Gas Mark 6.

Stir the chile, spices, chopped tomatoes, and thyme leaves into the onions and fennel in the pan. Cook over medium-low heat for 10–12 minutes. Stir in the spring greens and cook, covered with a lid, for 3 minutes until wilted. Mix the vegetable mixture into the quinoa and taste, adjusting the seasoning with more salt and pepper to taste.

Scoop the quinoa mixture into the four reserved pepper halves. (Any leftover quinoa makes a delicious accompaniment to some grilled halloumi or served alongside some crisp green salad leaves.)

Crumble the feta cheese over the peppers and return to the oven for 20 minutes, until the peppers are piping hot and the feta is melted. Serve at the center of a mezze selection.

Homemade Spicy Lamb Sausage

PREPARATION TIME
10 minutes + chilling time

COOKING TIME
10 minutes

MAKES
4 large sausages or
8 small sausages

- 14 oz/400 g ground (minced) lamb
- 2 garlic cloves, crushed
- 1½-inch/4-cm piece of fresh ginger, grated
- ½ teaspoon ground cinnamon
- 1 teaspoon ground cumin
- 1 teaspoon ground coriander
- ½ teaspoon ground allspice
- ½ teaspoon ground cloves
- ½ tsp paprika
- 1 teaspoon salt
- 1 teaspoon pepper
- 3 tablespoons fresh orange juice
- 5 tablespoons olive oil
- mixed salad, to serve
- Yogurt and Lemon Zest Dressing (see page 21), to serve (optional)

It's very easy to make your own sausages at home using good-quality ground (minced) meat. The grassy, gaminess of lamb pairs so well with some of my favorite spices, so I mix these into the lamb mixture to get a riot of flavor in every bite.

This recipe makes four large sausages, so it's a perfect dinner for two with a couple of other mezze, or make it for one and enjoy it in a wrap with a crunchy salad the following day.

PREPARATION

Using your hands, mix together the lamb, garlic, ginger, ground spices, paprika, salt, and pepper in a bowl until thoroughly combined. Gradually add the orange juice and 2 tablespoons of the olive oil and knead the mixture for 3–4 minutes. Cover the bowl with plastic wrap (clingfilm) and chill in the refrigerator overnight until firm.

The following day, shape finger-like sausages from the lamb mixture. Heat a skillet or frying pan and add the remaining oil. Add the sausages to the pan, in batches, and cook over medium heat, turning frequently, for 10 minutes. Serve hot with a mixed salad and some Yogurt and Lemon Zest Dressing (see page 21), if you like.

Chicken Livers with Garlic and Lemon Sauce

PREPARATION TIME
10 minutes

COOKING TIME
15 minutes

SERVES
4

14 oz/400 g chicken livers, diced
½ teaspoon salt
2 tablespoons olive oil

FOR GARLIC AND LEMON SAUCE
4 garlic cloves
⅔ cup (¼ pint/150 ml) extra virgin olive oil
juice ½ lemon
salt and pepper

Chicken livers are excellent value as well as being a rich source of protein, B vitamins, and vitamin A, which is important for healthy eye function. Although they've fallen out of fashion in favor of chicken breast and thigh, when cooked carefully alongside another strong flavor (like the garlic I use here), they make for a rewarding light lunch or weekday supper.

Ask your butcher to remove any sinew or irregular-colored parts of the liver as these can sometimes taste bitter if left on.

PREPARATION

Put the chicken livers into a dish, sprinkle with the salt, and toss well. Heat the olive oil a skillet or frying pan, add the chicken livers, and cook over medium heat, stirring frequently, for 15 minutes. Meanwhile, make the sauce. Crush the garlic with a pinch of salt in a mortar with a pestle. Add the oil olive and lemon juice and stir well. Season with salt and pepper.

Pour half the sauce over the liver and remove the pan from the heat. Transfer the liver mixture to a warm serving dish and serve immediately with the remaining sauce on the side.

Scrambled Egg with Salmon and Beets

PREPARATION TIME	COOKING TIME	SERVES
5 minutes	5–10 minutes	2

2 small flatbreads
4 eggs
2 tablespoons milk
2 teaspoons sumac
1 tablespoon butter
3 oz/80 g smoked salmon, cut into bite-size pieces
1 cooked beet (beetroot), diced
2 tablespoons chopped parsley
salt and pepper

This is a Middle Eastern twist on a Western breakfast classic of smoked salmon and scrambled eggs. I love the addition of earthy beet (beetroot) and lots of fresh herbs and sumac, which adds a bright citrus note.

Be sure to use a freshly cooked beet (you can buy vacuum-packed beets from most good stores), rather than the pickled beets you can buy in jars, which can be incredibly vinegary and won't add the richness to this indulgent breakfast that normal cooked beets will.

PREPARATION

Preheat the oven to 375°F/190°C/Gas Mark 5. Put the flatbreads into the oven for 5 minutes until crisp.

Meanwhile, lightly beat the eggs with the milk and sumac in a bowl, and season with salt and pepper. Melt the butter in a skillet or frying pan, pour in the egg mixture, and cook over medium-low heat, stirring with decreasing energy with a wooden spoon, until just set.

Tip the scrambled egg into a bowl and gently stir in the smoked salmon and beet (beetroot). Put a crisp flatbread on each of the 2 plates and divide the scrambled egg mixture between them. Sprinkle with the parsley and serve immediately.

Pan-Fried Sardines

PREPARATION TIME
10 minutes

COOKING TIME
4–5 minutes

SERVES
4

8 large sardines, scaled, cleaned, and head and fins removed
4 garlic cloves
½ teaspoon salt
3 tablespoons olive oil
juice of 1 lemon
salad greens (leaves), to serve

Sardines are rich in vitamins and essential Omega 3 fatty acids, which are helpful in supporting healthy heart function and thus preventing heart disease.

I pan fry these sardines quickly with garlic and lemon and serve them simply with a fresh salad to make a nutritious supper in minutes. Ask your fish supplier for the freshest sardines they have available and use a non-stick skillet or frying pan if you have one, to crisp up the sardine skins while you cook them.

PREPARATION

Open out the sardines like a book and place on a work surface skin side uppermost. Press firmly along the backbone of each fish with your thumb. Turn the fish over and carefully remove the backbones, snipping with scissors at the tail end. Trim the sides of the sardines and set aside in a dish.

Crush the garlic with the salt in a mortar with a pestle. Stir in the olive oil and lemon juice, then pour the mixture over the sardines and rub in on both sides.

Heat a heavy skillet or frying pan, add the sardines, skin side down, and cook for 2–3 minutes, then turn, and cook for another minute. Transfer the fish, skin side uppermost, to individual plates and serve immediately with salad greens (leaves).

Fried Sea Bass with Tahini and Curry Sauce

PREPARATION TIME	COOKING TIME	SERVES
10 minutes	10 minutes	2

4 sea bass fillets
1 tablespoon butter
1 teaspoon sesame seeds, toasted
2 tablespoons chopped cilantro (coriander)
salt and black pepper
squeeze of lemon juice, to serve

FOR THE SAUCE
6 tablespoons Tahini (see page 12)
1 teaspoon salt
juice of 1 lemon
1 teaspoon hot curry powder

Sea bass can stand up well to stronger flavors, and its relatively low fat content makes it a perfect match for this creamy and warming tahini and curry sauce.

Scoring the skin of the sea bass before cooking helps the seasonings to penetrate into the fillets, prevents the fillets from curling, and results in a delicious crisp-skinned fish.

Once you've cooked the fillets, serve them straight away as the fish is best eaten hot. I usually prepare this dish last as part of a mezze spread, to make sure it's as fresh as can be.

PREPARATION
Preheat the oven to 350°F/180°C/Gas Mark 4.

Mix together all sauce ingredients in a bowl and stir in ½ cup (4 fl oz/ 120 ml) water. Pour the sauce into an ovenproof dish and put in the oven to warm. Cut each fish fillet in half, score the skin with 2 slashes, and season with salt and pepper.

Heat a skillet or frying pan, add the butter, and when it has melted, add the fish, skin side down, and cook for about 2 minutes until the skin is golden and crispy. Turn the fillets over and cook for another 1–2 minutes until the flesh flakes easily.

Remove the dish from the oven, add the fish to the sauce, and sprinkle with the sesame seeds. Return the dish to the oven for 5 minutes. Remove from the oven, sprinkle the fish with chopped cilantro (coriander), add a squeeze of lemon juice, and serve immediately.

Cod Goujons with Garlic Dip

PREPARATION TIME
15 minutes

COOKING TIME
8–10 minutes

SERVES
4–6 (makes 18 goujons)

12 oz/350 g cod fillet, skinned
3 slices (3 oz/80 g) wheat (brown) bread, crusts removed
2 tablespoons snipped chives
pinch of paprika
4 tablespoons all-purpose (plain) flour
1 egg
3 tablespoons milk
sunflower oil, for deep-frying
salt and pepper
salad greens (leaves) to serve

FOR THE GARLIC DIP
4 garlic cloves
½ teaspoon sea salt
juice of ½ lemon
⅔ cup (5 fl oz/150 ml) thick plain (natural) yogurt
olive oil
pinch of ground sumac

When they were growing up, my grandchildren in London would often ask for fish fingers for dinner—and I admit that I was partial to their crispy breadcrumb shell and bung-it-in-the-oven-and-you're-done convenience.

These cod goujons were born out of a belief that I could make a frozen family favorite using fresh ingredients, and I really do think these are miles ahead of the freezer-aisle version in terms of flavor. I serve these with my garlic dip, which is lighter than a mayonnaise as it uses yogurt instead of eggs and oil.

PREPARATION
For the garlic dip, crush the garlic with the sea salt in a mortar with a pestle. Add the lemon juice and mix well. Stir the mixture into the yogurt in a small serving bowl, then chill in the refrigerator for 20 minutes. Just before serving, sprinkle over some olive oil and sumac.

Cut the fish into strips and set aside. Put the bread into a food processor and process to fine breadcrumbs. Tip the breadcrumbs onto a plate and stir in the chives and paprika.

Put the flour onto another plate, season with salt and pepper, and mix well. Lightly beat the egg with the milk in a shallow dish. Heat the oil in a deep-fryer to 350°F/180°C or until a cube of bread browns in 30 seconds.

Meanwhile, dip the fish strips in the flour, shaking off any excess, then in the egg mixture, and, finally, in the breadcrumbs. Add the fish strips to the hot oil, in batches, and fry for 8–10 minutes, until golden. Remove with a slotted spoon and drain on paper towels. Pile the goujons into a warm serving dish and serve immediately with garlic dip and salad greens (leaves).

CHAPTER SIX

Grains, Pulses & Rice

Saffron Rice and Vegetable Fatteh

PREPARATION TIME
20 minutes + 30 minutes soaking/salting time

COOKING TIME
40 minutes

SERVES
4–6 as small plates

pinch of saffron
1 ¾ cups (11 oz/300 g) basmati rice, well rinsed
2 large eggplant (aubergines), washed and cut into ½-inch/1-cm slices lengthwise
2 tablespoons butter or olive oil, plus extra for brushing
1 onion, peeled and finely chopped
4 garlic cloves, thinly sliced
1 cinnamon stick
4 large vine tomatoes, peeled and roughly chopped, or 1 (14-oz/400-g) can chopped tomatoes
2 Pita Breads (see page 200)
salt
1 small bunch parsley, leaves picked and coarsely chopped, to serve
¼ cup (2 oz/50 g) plain (natural) yogurt, to serve

Fatteh is a dish that everyone does their own way. In Lebanon we'll sometimes have it for breakfast, though I'm not sure if my English friends would ever do that! Traditionally it's a way of using up stale bread, which we'll top with anything from lamb to chickpeas to labneh. Here, I add eggplant (aubergine) and rice, finishing it with yogurt for a hearty meal.

PREPARATION

Soak the saffron in a small bowl with 3 tablespoons of warm water and set aside.

Soak the rice in plenty of cold salted water for a minimum of 30 minutes, covered with a dish towel.

Toss the eggplant (aubergine) slices with 1 heaping teaspoon salt and place in a colander set over a bowl for 20–30 minutes. This prevents the eggplant feeling woolly when cooked.

Preheat the oven to 425°F/220°C/Gas Mark 7.

Wipe the eggplant slices with paper towels, then toss with enough olive oil to coat and arrange in a single layer (without overlapping) on a baking sheet. Cook in the center of the oven for 15–20 minutes, until soft and golden. Set aside.

Meanwhile, melt the butter or warm the olive oil in a large saucepan with a lid over medium heat. Add the onion and a pinch of salt and sauté for 8–10 minutes, until soft, sweet, and just starting to color.

Drain the rice and add to the pan, along with the garlic, cinnamon, soaked saffron, and ½ teaspoon salt. Stir continuously to toast the rice for 2 minutes, then add the tomatoes and generous 2 cups (17 fl oz/500 ml) of water. Cover with the lid, turn the heat up to high and bring to the boil. Boil fast for 3 minutes, then turn the heat down to low, and cook for a further 10 minutes. Remove from the heat and let the rice rest for at least 5 minutes before serving.

Meanwhile, tear the pita into irregular-shaped triangles, about the size of tortilla chips, and brush with olive oil or melted butter. Arrange in a single layer on a baking sheet and bake in the oven for 5–7 minutes, until crispy.

Layer the toasted pita chips on a serving platter with the rice and eggplant (make 3 layers of each element). Sprinkle with the chopped parsley as you go. Serve topped with a dollop of yogurt.

Golden Bulgur Wheat with Crushed Roasted Carrots

PREPARATION TIME
15 minutes

COOKING TIME
50–60 minutes

SERVES
6

1 ¼ cups (7 oz/200 g) coarse bulgur wheat
½ vegetable bouillon (stock) cube
1 small thumb-sized piece turmeric, grated
⅓ cup (2 oz/50 g) skin-on almonds
12 oz/350 g carrots, cut into irregular ¾-inch/2-cm pieces
1 teaspoon fennel seeds
¼ teaspoon allspice
½ cucumber
½ red onion
2 tablespoons white wine vinegar
½ teaspoon salt
½ teaspoon golden superfine (caster) sugar
handful of mint, coarsely chopped
pomegranate seeds, to garnish (optional)
olive oil and lemon juice, to serve (optional)

This is a very colorful and traditionally flavored dish. Having raw red onion may seem like a stretch to some, but trust me when I tell you that when they are pickled alongside the cooling cucumber, the flavor is much less fiery and sharp. I like to eat this with a few slices of grilled halloumi and the Hibiscus and Mint Iced Tea (see page 260).

PREPARATION
Preheat the oven to 400°F/200°C/Gas Mark 6.

Cook the bulgur according to packet directions, crumbling in the bouillon (stock) cube and adding the grated turmeric before the pan comes to the boil.

Meanwhile, spread the almonds on a baking sheet and toast in the oven for 10 minutes. Remove from the oven, let cool slightly, then coarsely chop.

Meanwhile, put the chopped carrot in a roasting pan with ¼ cup (2 fl oz/60 ml) water, cover with aluminum foil and roast in the hot oven for 20 minutes. After this time, remove the pan from the oven, discard the foil and toss through the fennel seeds and allspice. Return the pan to the oven and roast for another 10–20 minutes.

While the carrot is cooking, slice the cucumber down the middle, remove the watery seeds with a teaspoon and discard. Cut the cucumber halves into ¼-inch/5-mm slices and put into a bowl. Thinly slice the red onion and put into the same bowl. Add the vinegar, salt, and sugar and squeeze the cucumber and onion to mix well with the pickling liquid. Set aside for 10 minutes.

When the carrots have finished cooking, arrange the golden bulgur on a serving platter. Crush the carrots with the back of a fork in their roasting pan, then arrange them on top of the bulgur. Lift the quick-pickled cucumber and onion out of the pickling liquid and squeeze to remove any excess vinegar. Scatter half over the top of the carrots and place the rest in a bowl on the side (people have varying levels of tolerance for pickles!).

Scatter the chopped almonds and mint over the top, along with the pomegranate seeds, if using. Serve immediately, dressed with a little olive oil and lemon juice if desired.

155

Butternut Squash, Cavolo Nero, and Freekeh

PREPARATION TIME
30 minutes

COOKING TIME
about 1 hour 30 minutes

SERVES
4 as a main or
6 as small plates

1 butternut squash (1 ¾ lb/ 800 g), peeled and seeded
zest and juice of 1 orange
1 teaspoon ground cinnamon
1 teaspoon cumin seeds
3 tablespoons olive oil
¾ cup (3 ½ oz/100 g) walnuts
2 tablespoons honey
scant 1 cup (7 oz/200 g) cracked or wholegrain freekeh, rinsed
2 tablespoons Tahini (see page 12)
1 tablespoon white wine vinegar
7 oz/200 g cavolo nero, roughly torn (stalks removed)
salt and pepper
pomegranate seeds, to serve

This is without a doubt one of the most popular recipes with friends and family in this book. Half of the sweet roasted squash is blitzed with tahini to make a creamy sauce, which pairs well with the nutty freekeh. Freekeh is widely available in Middle Eastern supermarkets and larger stores.

Freekeh has been around for thousands of years. It's made from green durum wheat that is roasted or smoked to give its distinct and very delicious flavor.

PREPARATION

Preheat the oven to 400°F/200°C/Gas Mark 6 and line a baking sheet with wax (greaseproof) paper.

Cut the squash into ¾-inch/2-cm cubes and put into a roasting pan with the orange zest and juice, spices, salt, pepper, and 1 tablespoon olive oil. Mix well, cover tightly with aluminum foil and place in the center of the oven for 30 minutes.

Coarsely chop the walnuts and mix them in a bowl with 1 tablespoon water, the honey, and a pinch of salt. Spread them over a lined baking sheet and roast in the oven for 6-8 minutes, turning half-way through and taking care not to let them burn. Set aside to cool.

After 30 minutes, remove the foil and test with a knife—the squash should be soft all the way through. If not, re-cover and return to the oven for a further 5–10 minutes. Set the squash aside to cool.

While the squash and walnuts are roasting, put the freekeh in a saucepan with 1 ⅔ cups (14 fl oz/400 ml) cold water, a good pinch of salt, and 1 tablespoon olive oil. Cover with a lid and bring to the boil over medium heat. Turn the heat down to a simmer and cook until the grains become tender, adding more water, if necessary. This will take 10–15 minutes for cracked freekeh and up to 45 minutes for wholegrain freekeh. When cooked, drain off any excess water and let the freekeh cool slightly.

To make the dressing, place one-quarter of the cooked squash in a mixing bowl, along with the tahini, vinegar, 2 tablespoons olive oil, and a good pinch of salt and pepper. Puree in a food processor or with an immersion (stick) blender, until creamy. Taste and adjust seasoning.

Toss the cavolo nero through the remaining cooked squash and return to the oven (without the foil) for 5 minutes, until the cavolo nero has wilted and crisped up, and the squash is catching at the edges.

Put the cooked freekeh into a serving bowl and pour the dressing over. Add the squash and cavolo nero and toss it all together. Sprinkle over the walnuts and pomegranate seeds to serve.

Fasolia

PREPARATION TIME	COOKING TIME	SERVES
30 minutes	2 hours	4–6 as small plates

⅔ cups (5 fl oz/150 ml) olive oil, plus extra for frying
2 small white onions, finely chopped
6 large vine tomatoes
1 ½ cups (7 oz/200 g) frozen fava (broad) beans
6 garlic cloves, finely sliced
1 lb/450 g fine green beans, trimmed and halved crosswise
1 small bunch dill
salt and pepper

Many countries claim ownership of this delicious stew and argue that theirs is where its origins lie. Fasolia can be found in the countries surrounding the Red Sea to the Mediterranean; from Ethiopia to Greece. This dish is usually a combination of beans, onion, and tomato wherever it is made in the world, with each country adding its unique twist. I've used a mixture of string (French) beans and frozen fava (broad) beans here. I like the texture after they've been braised slowly for a long time—the oil breaks down the tough skin of the beans, making them as delicious to eat on their own as well as part of a mezze selection.

PREPARATION
In a deep saucepan, warm a splash of olive oil over medium heat and fry the onions with a pinch of salt for 8–10 minutes, stirring regularly, until soft, sweet, and translucent.

Meanwhile, boil some water. With a serrated knife, cut a cross in the skin on the bottom of the tomatoes, without cutting too deep into the flesh. Place the tomatoes in a medium-sized bowl and cover with the boiling water. After 2 minutes, remove from the water and leave to cool. Place the frozen fava (broad) beans in a separate bowl, cover with boiling water and set aside.

Add the garlic to the pan with the onions for 2 minutes, or until it just starts to color. Turn the heat off while you prepare the tomatoes.

By now the tomatoes should be cool enough to handle. Working from the cross at the base, peel the skin away from each tomato. Slice each tomato in half from top to bottom, cut out and discard the tough white core in a deep 'V' slice, then coarsely chop the tomatoes and add to the pan with the onions and garlic. Add the green beans, season generously with salt and pepper, then stir in the olive oil. Turn the heat down low.

Meanwhile, drain the fava beans. If you have time, pop them out of their skins to reveal the little emerald beans hidden inside the lighter green shells. This will feel like a lot of effort, but trust me when I say it makes for the most delicious flavor and texture eventually. When you've podded the beans, add them to the pan with the other vegetables and stir to combine.

Cook over the lowest heat possible for at least 2 hours, stirring very occasionally. If it looks as though it's catching at the bottom, add 3–6 tablespoons water. Keep an eye on it and if it still looks like it's catching, cover the pan. The beans are ready when they are almost silky soft when you eat one. Sprinkle the dill over the top and serve warm or at room temperature, but never chilled.

Toasted Quinoa with Beets, Olives, and Orange

PREPARATION TIME
10 minutes

COOKING TIME
35–40 minutes

SERVES
4 as small plates

¾ cup (5 oz/150 g) quinoa, rinsed under cold running water
pinch of salt
5 oz/150 g raw beets (beetroot), peeled and grated
1 small bunch parsley, leaves picked and reserved, stalks finely chopped
¾ cup (2 ¾ oz/70 g) mixed olives, pitted and halved
1 tablespoon olive oil
⅓ cup (2 oz/50 g) walnuts
zest of ½ orange
Greek yogurt, to serve
green salad, to serve

Beetroot and orange is a combination I really love in both sweet and savory dishes. This is a vibrant quick dinner I'll often make for guests who can't eat gluten.

PREPARATION

Heat a large skillet or frying pan over medium–low heat, add the rinsed quinoa and toast for about 20 minutes, stirring regularly. At first, a lot of steam will be released as the quinoa dries out, but the grains will eventually turn a deep golden color, and start popping and smelling nutty. It's important to stir regularly to ensure that the quinoa toasts evenly and doesn't burn.

When the quinoa is well toasted, stir through the grated beets (beetroot), along with a pinch of salt. Cook for 2–3 minutes, then add the parsley stalks, olives, and olive oil to the pan. Pour in 1 ¼ cups (10 ½ fl oz/300 ml) of hot water to cover, then turn the heat up to medium–high. Cook for 10–15 minutes, until all the water has evaporated and the quinoa is tender.

Meanwhile, heat a small skillet or frying pan over medium heat. Toast the walnuts for 5 minutes, shaking the pan occasionally, until light golden on the inside when broken. Cool slightly, then coarsely chop and set aside.

When the quinoa is cooked, stir through the orange zest, then arrange on a serving dish. Coarsely chop the reserved parsley leaves and sprinkle them over the top, along with the chopped walnuts.

Serve with some Greek yogurt and a green salad alongside.

Eggplant Rice Rolls

PREPARATION TIME
25 minutes + 20 minutes rice cooling time

COOKING TIME
50 minutes

SERVES
4 as small plates

FOR THE FILLING
- ½ cup (3 ½ oz/100 g) long-grain brown rice
- ½ (14-oz/400-g) can chickpeas, drained
- 1 ½ teaspoons Za'atar (see page 13)
- ½ teaspoon Lebanese 7-Spice Seasoning (see page 12)
- large handful of cilantro (coriander) or parsley, washed and coarsely chopped
- salt

FOR THE GRILLED EGGPLANT
- 1 large eggplant (aubergine), top removed, cut into ½-inch/1-cm slices lengthwise
- 1 ½ tablespoons olive oil
- ½ teaspoon salt

FOR THE LEMON TAHINI SAUCE
- zest and juice of 1 lemon
- 1 garlic clove, minced
- 2 ½ tablespoons Tahini (see page 12)
- 4 tablespoons extra virgin olive oil
- 2 tablespoons water
- 1 teaspoon honey
- salt and pepper

Baked chickpeas and rice crisp up nicely in the oven, and are delicious alongside these delicate eggplant (aubergine) rolls. I added a quick tahini dressing to bring it all together. If your tahini separates, try whizzing up this sauce in a food processor or blender.

The key to success with this dish is to cook the eggplants (aubergines) through so that they're soft and not woolly. They'll hold the filling better in the roasting tray and taste so delicious when they've been cooked twice like this.

PREPARATION

Bring 1 cup (8 fl oz/250 ml) salted water to the boil in a saucepan and add the rice. Cover and return to the boil. Reduce heat to medium, then simmer for 30 minutes, or until the rice is tender but retains a little bite. Drain, then let cool for about 10 minutes.

Meanwhile, heat a large skillet or frying pan over medium-high heat. Drizzle the eggplant (aubergine) slices with the olive oil and sprinkle evenly with the salt. Fry each slice for 5–8 minutes, turning once, until softened. Remove from the pan and set aside on paper towels to drain off any excess oil.

For the lemon tahini sauce, in a small bowl, mix together the lemon zest, juice, and garlic. Let sit for 5 minutes for the garlic to mellow. Whisk in the tahini, olive oil, water, honey and a pinch of salt and pepper to taste. Set aside.

In a large mixing bowl, combine the cooled rice, chickpeas, spices, most of the cilantro (coriander) or parsley (reserve a little for garnish), ½ teaspoon salt, and half of the lemon tahini sauce. Stir until well combined.

Preheat the oven to 400°F/200°C/Gas Mark 6 and grease a roasting dish lightly with oil. On your work surface, lay out a sheet of parchment (baking) paper for rolling.

Lay the fried eggplant slices on the parchment paper. Put a heaping dessertspoonful of the filling mixture onto one end of each eggplant slice (you do not need to use up all the filling mixture). Use the parchment paper to roll the slices up to encase the filling, brushing with a little lemon tahini sauce as you go, to help the slices stick. Nestle the rolls together in the roasting dish, seam-side down. Sprinkle the remaining rice and chickpea filling around the edges of the dish. Bake for 20 minutes.

Remove from the oven and drizzle with the remaining lemon tahini sauce. Sprinkle with the reserved chopped herbs and serve.

Wild Rice Salad with Roasted Root Vegetables

PREPARATION TIME
25 minutes + 20 minutes cooling time

COOKING TIME
40 minutes

SERVES
6–8 as small plates

- 4 raw, unpeeled baby beets (beetroot), scrubbed (if you can't get baby beets, use 2 smallish beets, cut in half)
- 2 teaspoons olive oil, plus extra for drizzling
- 2 teaspoons balsamic vinegar
- 7 oz/200 g celery root (celeriac), peeled and cut into ¾-inch/2-cm cubes
- 7 oz/200 g carrots, peeled and "roll cut" (see explanation above)
- 3 ½ oz/100 g turnip or swede, peeled and cut into ¾-inch/2-cm cubes
- 1 cup (7 oz/200 g) wild rice, rinsed well under cold water
- ½ vegetable bouillon (stock) cube
- 1 small bunch mixed soft herbs (I use parsley, mint, and dill), coarsely chopped
- salt and pepper

FOR THE DRESSING
- 2 tablespoons Tahini (see page 12)
- 2 tablespoons harissa
- 4 tablespoons olive oil
- 1 teaspoon honey
- zest and juice of 1 lemon
- pinch each of salt and pepper

Wild rice is something I've bought more of in London than in Lebanon. Though it takes a little while to cook, it has a delicious nutty flavor and a very satisfying texture. Well-seasoned vegetables make it into a substantial bowl for a mezze spread.

Roll cutting a cylindrical vegetable gives even-sized pieces and exposes as much surface area to the heat as possible, so the pieces cook quickly and evenly. To roll cut, start at the top, make a diagonal cut, then roll the carrot away from you a quarter turn and cut again, keeping the knife at the same angle. I think of it as cutting 3D triangles.

PREPARATION
Preheat the oven to 375°F/190°C/Gas Mark 5.

Place each beet (beetroot) in the center of a 4 x 4-inch/10 x 10-cm square of aluminum foil. Evenly distribute the olive oil and balsamic vinegar (you want about ½ teaspoon of each in each foil parcel), season with salt and pepper, then close each square by folding up all 4 corners to the middle and twisting to seal. Place on a small baking sheet and roast in the center of the oven for 40 minutes.

Meanwhile, on a larger baking sheet, toss the celery root (celeriac), carrots, and turnips with a drizzle of olive oil.

In a small bowl, mix together the dressing ingredients. Drizzle half of the mixture over the chopped root vegetables on the baking sheet and toss well to coat. Set the remaining dressing aside.

Cover the vegetables with aluminum foil and roast in the oven for 30 minutes, removing the foil after 20 minutes.

Meanwhile, place the wild rice in a large saucepan with 2 cups (16 fl oz/475 ml) of boiling water and crumble in the bouillon (stock) cube. Bring to the boil and cook for 10 minutes over high heat. Cover the pan with the lid, turn the heat down to medium, and cook for a further 15–20 minutes, until all the water has evaporated and the rice is fluffy.

Add the chopped herbs to the remaining dressing. When the rice is cooked and still warm, mix the dressing through the rice with a fork and set aside. The rice will absorb the lovely flavors as it cools.

Remove the baking sheets from the oven. Carefully open the beet parcels to release the steam and let cool.

When the beets are cool enough to handle, rub the skins off under cold water, then chop into chunks about the size of the roasted vegetables. Mix everything together in a mixing bowl and check the seasoning. Serve at room temperature, or still slightly warm.

Lentils with Slow-Roasted Tomatoes and Thyme

PREPARATION TIME
5 minutes

COOKING TIME
50 minutes

SERVES
4 as small plates

FOR THE TOMATOES
2 ⅔ cups (14 oz/400 g) cherry tomatoes
few sprigs of thyme
1 tablespoon olive oil
1 teaspoon balsamic vinegar
salt and pepper

FOR THE LENTILS
scant 1 cup (7 oz/200 g) Puy lentils
2 large tomatoes, coarsely chopped, or 8 cherry tomatoes, halved
1 bay leaf
few sprigs of thyme
1 garlic clove, peeled
3 tablespoons olive oil
salt and pepper
Labneh (see page 10), to serve

Lentils are such a comfort food for me, especially when stirred with slow-roasted, collapsed tomatoes and fragrant thyme.

PREPARATION
Preheat the oven to 325°F/160°C/Gas Mark 3.
   Arrange half of the cherry tomatoes on a baking sheet with half of the thyme sprigs. Drizzle over half the olive oil and balsamic vinegar, and sprinkle over some salt and pepper. Roast in the center of the oven for 10 minutes.
   Meanwhile, halve the remaining tomatoes around the middle.
   Remove the baking sheet from the oven and add the halved tomatoes with the rest of the thyme, olive oil, vinegar, and a little more salt and pepper. Ensure everything is evenly seasoned. Roast for a further 30 minutes.
   Rinse the lentils in a strainer (sieve) under cold running water, then place in a medium saucepan and cover with fresh water. Add the tomatoes, bay leaf, thyme, and garlic, then bring to the boil over medium-high heat. Cook for 15–20 minutes, until the lentils are soft. Drain any excess liquid, then stir in the olive oil and season well with salt and pepper.
   Stir the halved slow-roasted cherry tomatoes through the lentils, scatter the whole slow-roasted tomatoes over the top and serve with labneh on the side.

Spiced Red Lentil Koftas

PREPARATION TIME
20 minutes

COOKING TIME
25 minutes

SERVES
4–6 (makes 12 koftas)

FOR THE KOFTAS
- 3 tablespoons extra virgin olive oil
- 2 shallots or 1 small red onion, finely chopped
- 3 garlic cloves, finely chopped
- 1 egg, beaten
- 1 cup (9 oz/250 g) cooked red lentils
- 1 teaspoon dried oregano
- 1 small bunch parsley, coarsely chopped
- 1 tablespoon tomato paste (purée)
- 2 oz/50 g halloumi, finely grated
- pinch of dried chili flakes
- scant 1 cup (2 oz/50 g) breadcrumbs
- salt
- crunchy salad, to serve (optional)

FOR THE CITRUS YOGURT SAUCE
- 4 tablespoons thick Greek yogurt
- 1 tablespoon Tahini (see page 12)
- 1 teaspoon date molasses or honey
- zest and juice of ½ lemon
- few sprigs of cilantro (coriander), leaves picked and chopped
- few sprigs of parsley, leaves picked and chopped

The patties in my last book went down so well I wanted to include some fresh ideas here. Red lentils are really moreish when baked this way, with plenty of garlic and shallots for flavor.

PREPARATION

Preheat the oven to 400°F/200°C/Gas Mark 6. Line a baking sheet with parchment (baking) paper.

Heat 1 tablespoon of the olive oil in a medium skillet or frying pan over medium heat. Add the shallot or onion with a pinch of salt, and cook for 5 minutes until starting to soften. Add the garlic and cook for 2 minutes, without letting the shallot or garlic burn. Remove from the heat and let cool for a few minutes.

In a large mixing bowl, combine the cooked shallot and garlic with the other kofta ingredients and mix well. Taste and adjust the seasoning.

Half-fill a small bowl with water and, moistening your fingers as you go, take heaping tablespoons of the mixture, and roll into golf-ball sized koftas by hand.

Heat the remaining olive oil in a large skillet or frying pan over medium–high heat and fry the koftas, turning frequently, for about 5 minutes, or until brown all over. Remove to the prepared baking sheet with a slotted spoon and bake in the oven for 10 minutes.

Meanwhile, in a small bowl, mix together the ingredients for the citrus yogurt sauce.

Serve the koftas with the citrus yogurt sauce in a bowl on the side and a crunchy salad.

Whole Baked Squash with Quinoa

PREPARATION TIME
10 minutes

COOKING TIME
1 hour 25 minutes

SERVES
6–8

1 butternut squash (about 1 ¾ lb/800 g)
olive oil, for drizzling
1 sweet pointed (Romano) red pepper, seeded and cut into slim ¾-inch/2-cm pieces, lengthwise
⅔ cup (3 ½ oz/100 g) quinoa
1 red chile, finely chopped
1 small bunch parsley, coarsely chopped
3 ½ oz/100 g feta cheese, crumbled
½ teaspoon cinnamon
⅓ cup (2 oz/50 g) pine nuts
1 teaspoon dried mint
zest of 1 lemon, plus a squeeze of lemon juice to serve (optional)
salt and pepper
green salad, to serve

See pages 172–173 for image

This is such a celebratory way to serve squash and is a wonderful centerpiece to a mezze spread. It's satisfying too with lots of different textures from the sweet, yielding squash to the crispy quinoa stuffing. I usually serve each squash in quarters, including the skin too (which is edible). Over the last few years, I've been experimenting with quinoa instead of rice having learnt that quinoa contains all the essential amino acids (those which can't be produced by the human body) in a healthy balance.

PREPARATION
Preheat the oven to 350°F/180°C/Gas Mark 4.

Cut the butternut squash in half lengthwise and scoop out the seeds. Place the squash cut-side up in a roasting pan, drizzle with olive oil, and sprinkle with salt and pepper. Roast in the oven for 50 minutes, until the squash is soft.

Meanwhile, toss the sweet pepper in enough olive oil to coat, sprinkle with salt and pepper, then place in the oven for the last 10 minutes of the squash's roasting time, turning the oven up to 400°F/200°C/Gas Mark 6.

While the squash is roasting, cook the quinoa according to the packet directions and drain.

Remove the squash from the oven and scoop out some of the flesh, but leave about ½ inch/1 cm of flesh around the skin. Place the softened squash in a mixing bowl and mash with a fork. Mix with the remaining ingredients, including the roasted pepper, then taste and adjust the seasoning.

Spoon the stuffing back into the squash and drizzle with olive oil. Return to the oven for 25–30 minutes.

Serve with green salad and a squeeze of lemon, if desired.

Baked Farro with Feta, Herbs, and Olives

PREPARATION TIME
15 minutes

COOKING TIME
1 hour

SERVES
6 as small plates

olive oil, for frying
2 red onions, finely chopped
pinch of salt
⅔ cup (3 oz/80 g) Kalamata olives, pitted
1 sweet pointed (Romano) red pepper, cut into long ½-inch/1-cm-wide pieces, then into ¾-inch/2-cm lengths
2 garlic cloves, finely chopped
1 (14-oz/400-g) can chopped tomatoes
2 teaspoons ras-el-hanout
1 tablespoon sherry vinegar
1¼ cups (9 oz/250 g) farro
1 small bunch thyme
3 oz/80 g feta cheese
⅓ cup (1 oz/25 g) slivered (flaked) almonds
few sprigs of dill and/or parsley, to serve

See pages 172–173 for image

This is a dish I crave when feeling under the weather. The addition of the luxury ras-el-hanout (which means 'top of the shop'), with its heady mix of rose, and up to 100 different spices depending on where you buy it from, feels indulgent alongside the crunchy flaked almonds in this dish. Ras-el-hanout is used in a myriad of dishes in the Middle East and as such is often described as the garam masala (a classic Indian spice blend) of the Middle East.

I use black kale here (or cavolo nero), but curly kale, which has a shorter growing season, will work well too.

PREPARATION

Heat a splash of olive oil in a large ovenproof skillet or frying pan over medium heat. Add the red onions and a pinch of salt and cook, stirring regularly, for 8–10 minutes, until the onion turns sweet and translucent.

Meanwhile, preheat the oven to 400°F/200°C/Gas Mark 6. Coarsely chop half of the olives, leave the other half whole.

Turn the heat up to medium-high, add the sweet pepper and a pinch of salt and cook, stirring regularly, for another 4 minutes, or until the slices are just starting to soften and catch a little at the edges. Add a splash of water if you think they're about to burn. Stir in the garlic, tomatoes (keep the can), ras-el-hanout, and sherry vinegar. Fill the tomato can with water twice, adding both to the pan. Stir in the farro, the chopped and whole olives, and half of the thyme sprigs. Turn the heat to high, bring to the boil, then carefully transfer the pan to the preheated oven for 30 minutes.

Remove from the oven—it should still have some patches which are more liquid than others but don't worry, the farro grains will absorb most of the residual liquid. Crumble the feta cheese over the top in small chunks, then scatter over the slivered (flaked) almonds, and the remaining sprigs of thyme. Return to the oven for 10 minutes.

Meanwhile, chop the dill and parsley. Remove the pan from the oven and scatter over the herbs. Serve hot in the pan at the table.

172 GRAINS, PULSES & RICE

1. Ful Medames (p.175) 2. Seeded Couscous Tabbouleh (p.174) 3. Whole Baked Squash with Quinoa (p.170) 4. Baked Farro with Feta, Herbs, and Olives (p.171)

Seeded Couscous Tabbouleh

PREPARATION TIME
30 minutes

COOKING TIME
5 minutes

SERVES
6–8

2 cups (11 oz/300 g) couscous
½ vegetable bouillon (stock) cube
3 large tomatoes
1 red onion, finely chopped
few sprigs each of soft herbs, such as cilantro (coriander), dill, parsley, or mint, coarsely chopped
3½ oz/100 g mixed seeds (I like to use a mixture of sunflower, pumpkin, and sesame), toasted

FOR THE DRESSING
3 tablespoons olive oil
zest and juice of 1 orange
zest and juice of 1 lemon
1 teaspoon Dijon mustard
1 teaspoon honey
salt and pepper

See pages 172–173 for image

Adding vegetable bouillon (stock) to grains, pulses, and rice is such an easy way to add layers of flavor; I usually only use half a cube though, as often they can be very salty. When cooking with nuts and seeds, I always try to toast them gently to release the oils, which is where most of the flavor is.

PREPARATION
Put the couscous into a bowl and crumble the bouillon (stock) cube over the top, then cover with 2 ½ cups (20 fl oz/600 ml) boiling water. Cover and set aside for 6 minutes.

Cut a small cross into the base of each tomato, just slightly breaking the skin. Put the tomatoes into a bowl and pour over enough boiling water to cover. Cover and set aside for 5 minutes.

Meanwhile, make the dressing. Mix together all of the ingredients in a medium bowl. Taste and adjust the seasoning.

Fluff up the couscous with a fork, then transfer to a large serving bowl.

Drain the tomatoes, then peel away the skins and discard. Cut the skinned tomatoes into quarters, scooping out and discarding the seeds and pith. Coarsely chop the tomato flesh, mix with the couscous, then stir through the red onion and chopped herbs. Finally, mix through the toasted seeds and dressing.

Ful Medames

PREPARATION TIME
5 minutes

COOKING TIME
5–10 minutes

SERVES
4

2 (14-oz/400-g) cans ful medames (cooked fava beans)
2 garlic cloves, minced
2 teaspoons ground cumin
1 small bunch parsley, leaves coarsely chopped
juice of 1 lemon
olive oil, to drizzle
sea salt and pepper
Arabic flatbread or Pita Bread (see page 200), to serve

See pages 172–173 for image

One of the definitive dishes of Middle Eastern cuisine, Ful Medames is a bean stew lightly spiced with cumin that is often eaten at breakfast, to wake up the taste buds. It's my husband Heni's favorite, but is also excellent as part of a mezze. The tins of cooked fava beans in Middle Eastern stores are well worth hunting out, where they will be called "Ful Medames".

PREPARATION
Drain half the liquid from each can of ful medames (cooked fava beans). Transfer to a saucepan set over medium heat and bring to the boil. Cook for 5–10 minutes, then remove from the heat and stir in the garlic, cumin, most of the parsley (reserve a little for garnish), and lemon juice.

Transfer to a serving bowl, drizzle with olive oil, season generously, and sprinkle with the reserved parsley. Serve with plenty of bread.

Quick Orzo with Kale and Sumac

PREPARATION TIME	COOKING TIME	SERVES
10 minutes	30 minutes	4

2 tablespoons olive oil
2 leeks, washed and finely shredded
3 garlic cloves, coarsely chopped
1 (14-oz/400-g) can chopped tomatoes
1 tablespoon harissa
1 tablespoon ground sumac
1 teaspoon nigella seeds
1 cinnamon stick
7 oz/200 g dried orzo pasta
1 ½ cups (3 ½ oz/100 g) kale, washed, leaves stripped from stems and roughly chopped
extra virgin olive oil, to serve
7 oz/200 g feta cheese, to serve
salt and pepper

Orzo is the little rice-shaped pasta that's widely used from Italy across to Turkey. Here I cook it in the sauce so the starch from the pasta lends a richness to the spicy tomatoes as everything cooks together. Nigella seeds are also known as black onion seeds, but they look like black sesame seeds. They add such an interesting flavor and look so pretty dotted through the bright red sauce.

PREPARATION
Heat the olive oil in a large, deep skillet or frying pan over medium heat. Add the leeks and a pinch of salt and cook, stirring frequently, for 10 minutes until the leeks are soft and beginning to take on some color. Add the garlic, tomatoes (keep the can), harissa, sumac, nigella seeds, and cinnamon, stir to combine and cook for 5 minutes, until the sauce has thickened and reduced. Stir in the orzo, then fill the tomato can with water twice, adding both to the pan. Return to a simmer and cook for 10 minutes, until most of the water has been absorbed, but the orzo is still very al dente. Stir through the kale and cook for a further 3–4 minutes, until the kale is wilted and the orzo is cooked through.

Check the seasoning, and serve generously drizzled with olive oil and with the feta cheese crumbled over the top.

Lentil and Bulgur Wheat M'juderah

PREPARATION TIME	COOKING TIME	SERVES
10 minutes + 30 minutes soaking time	40–45 minutes	4

½ cup (3 ½ oz/100 g) coarse bulgur wheat
4 tablespoons sunflower oil
5 onions: 3 sliced and 2 cut into rings
1 ¼ cups (9 oz/250 g) dried Puy or green lentils, rinsed
½ teaspoon ground cumin
½ teaspoon ground coriander
1 teaspoon Lebanese 7-Spice Seasoning (see page 12)
salt and pepper

M'juderah is a gentle and calming combination of lentils and spiced, crispy onions and isn't a world away from the Indian Ayurvedic rice and lentil dish, kitchari. It's certainly a dish that I turn to when I want comforting, and indeed, I must have made it hundreds of times since I was a young girl in Lebanon.

PREPARATION

Soak the bulgur wheat in boiling water for 30 minutes, then drain and squeeze out any excess water.

Heat 1 ½ tablespoons of sunflower oil in a large skillet or frying pan over medium heat. Add the sliced onions and sauté for about 20 minutes, until soft and golden.

Add the lentils and the spices to the onions, then sauté for another minute. Cover with 2 ½ cups (20 fl oz/600 ml) of boiling water, and cook for about 20 minutes, until the lentils are tender (adding more water, if necessary).

Add the bulgur wheat to the pan and stir to combine. Season well with salt and pepper, then set aside and keep warm.

Heat the remaining 2 ½ tablespoons of sunflower oil in a large skillet or frying pan over medium heat. Add the onion rings and sauté for about 8 minutes, until crispy and caramelized. Drain on paper towels.

Serve the m'juderah topped with the crispy onion rings.

Upside Down Eggplants

PREPARATION TIME	COOKING TIME	SERVES
15 minutes + cooling time	1 hour	12

2 large eggplants (aubergines), cut lengthwise into ¼ inch/5 mm thick slices
1 tablespoon olive oil, plus extra for brushing
1 lb 2 oz/500 g ground (minced) lamb
1 onion, sliced
½ teaspoon ground cinnamon
½ teaspoon ground allspice
½ teaspoon ground cumin
1 tablespoon tomato paste (purée)
2 ½ cups (1 pint/600 ml) hot vegetable stock
1 cup (7 oz/200 g) basmati rice, rinsed
1 cinnamon stick
¼ cup (1 oz/25 g) pine nuts, toasted
¼ cup (1 oz/25 g) slivered (flaked) almonds, toasted
salt and pepper
thick Greek yogurt, to serve (optional)

This is a real centerpiece of a dish; griddle-charred eggplants encasing a spiced lamb and rice filling are baked, before being sprinkled with toasted nuts and sliced into generous wedges.

It took me a while to learn to be patient when using the ridged grill (griddle) pan, but if you resist moving things around too much, you'll be rewarded with distinct griddle marks and a delicious smoky flavor.

The recipe makes enough to serve 12, so make it for a large gathering or stuff any extras into pitas with a salad the next day.

PREPARATION

Preheat the oven to 375°F/190°C/Gas Mark 5 and heat a ridged grill (griddle) pan. Brush each eggplant (aubergine) slice with olive oil, put them in the hot grill pan, in batches, and cook for a few minutes on each side or until slightly golden and stripy. Once they have all been cooked, put them on a plate, season with salt and pepper, and set aside. Heat the oil in a skillet or frying pan, add the lamb, and cook over medium heat, stirring frequently, for 8–10 minutes until evenly browned. Add the onion, reduce the heat, and cook, stirring occasionally, for another 5 minutes until softened. Stir in the cinnamon, allspice, cumin, and tomato paste (purée) and season with salt and pepper. Pour in scant 1 cup (7 fl oz/200 ml) of the hot stock, mix well, and simmer over low heat for 10 minutes. Remove the pan from the heat and set aside. Meanwhile, put the rice into a pan, pour in 1¼ cups (½ pint/300 ml) of the remaining hot stock, and add the cinnamon stick. Bring to a boil over medium heat, then reduce the heat, cover, and simmer for 10 minutes or until all the stock has been absorbed and the rice is tender. Remove the pan from the heat and discard the cinnamon stick.

Line the bottom and sides of an 8 inch/20 cm round cake pan with some of the eggplant slices. Add half the lamb, followed by half the rice. Add another layer of eggplant slices, then the remaining lamb, followed by the remaining rice. Pour in the remaining stock and cover the top with eggplant slices. Cover the cake pan with foil, put it onto baking sheet, and bake for 20 minutes. Remove the foil, return the cake pan to the oven, and bake for another 10 minutes. Remove the pan from the oven and let cool for 10 minutes, then turn out onto a serving plate. (Put plate upside down over the cake pan and, holding them together, invert them.) Sprinkle with the pine nuts and almonds to serve, and Greek yogurt, if using.

Large Chicken Kibbeh with Apricots

PREPARATION TIME
20 minutes + soaking time

COOKING TIME
20–30 minutes

SERVES
8

1 large onion
2¼ lb/1 kg skinless boneless chicken breasts
generous 2 cups (11 oz/300 g) bulgur wheat, soak in water for 10 minutes and squeeze out in cheesecloth (muslin)
1 teaspoon Lebanese 7-Spice Seasoning (see page 12)
2 teaspoons ground cumin
2 teaspoons pepper
¾ cup (3½ oz/100 g) dried apricots, chopped
2 beets (beetroots), grated
olive oil, for brushing and drizzling
salt

Kibbeh is a classic Lebanese dish, usually made with a mixture of bulgur wheat, meat, and Middle Eastern spices (although there are many wonderful vegetarian variations). It can either be shaped into individual, falafel-sized pieces, or baked as a whole, like a pie before being sliced into diamonds or wedges.

This kibbeh is made using lean chicken and is a delicious alternative to a chicken pie.

PREPARATION

Put the onion and chicken into a food processor and process until finely ground (minced), then tip into a bowl. Add the bulgur wheat, spice seasoning, cumin, pepper, apricots, and beets (beetroots), season well with salt, and knead until thoroughly combined.

Preheat the oven to 400°F/200°C/Gas Mark 6. Brush a 12 inch/ 30 cm round cake pan with a little oil and put it into the oven to warm for 5 minutes. Firmly press the chicken mixture into the prepared pan, score the top into 8 portions, and drizzle with oil. Bake for 20–30 minutes.

Slice along score lines and serve.

Large Lamb Kibbeh

PREPARATION TIME	COOKING TIME	SERVES
30 minutes + soaking time	1 hour 30 minutes	8

1 x 1¾ lb/800 g half leg of lamb
1 large onion, coarsely chopped
1 teaspoon Lebanese 7-Spice Seasoning (see page 12)
1 teaspoons ground cumin
1 teaspoon pepper
1 teaspoon dried mint
3⅓ cups (1¼ lb/570 g) bulgur wheat, soaked in water for 10 minutes and squeeze out in cheesecloth (muslin)
olive oil, for brushing and drizzling

FOR THE FILLING
1 teaspoon olive oil
1 lb 2 oz/500 g ground (minced) lamb
2 onions, chopped
¾ cup (3 oz/80 g) pine nuts, toasted
1 teaspoon Lebanese 7-Spice Seasoning (see page 12)
1 teaspoon pepper
1 teaspoon salt
1 teaspoon ground coriander
1 teaspoon ground cinnamon

Like the Large Chicken Kibbeh with Apricots on page 182, this is made using a combination of meat and bulgur wheat. Here, I make a pine nut and gently spiced lamb filling to sit between two layers of lamb and bulgur kibbeh, which gives a lovely textural contrast.

The recipe will serve 8, but as part of a mezze is likely to go much further, although any leftovers will keep covered in the refrigerator for up to a week. I like to serve this kibbeh alongside a couple of salads and the Yogurt and Lemon Zest Dressing on page 21.

PREPARATION
First make the filling. Heat the oil in a skillet or frying pan, add the lamb, and cook over medium heat, stirring frequently for 8–10 minutes until evenly browned. Reduce the heat, add the onions, and cook, stirring occasionally for another 5 minutes. Stir in the pine nuts, spice seasoning, pepper, salt, ground coriander, and cinnamon and cook for a few more minutes. Remove the pan from the heat.

Trim the fat from the lamb, then cut the meat off the bone. Put it into a food processor with the onion and process until finely ground (minced). Tip it into a bowl, add the spice seasoning, cumin, pepper, mint, and bulgur wheat, and knead until thoroughly mixed.

Preheat the oven to 400°F/200°C/Gas Mark 6. Brush a 12 inch/ 30 cm round cake pan with a little oil and put it into the oven to warm for 5 minutes. Divide the mixture in half and firmly press one half into the prepared pan. Add the filling, then cover with the remaining lamb and bulgur wheat mixture, pressing firmly. Score the top into 8 portions, or with a diamond pattern, and drizzle with oil. Bake for 50 minutes, slice and then serve immediately.

CHAPTER SEVEN

Pastries & Breads

Favorite Manoushe with New Toppings

PREPARATION TIME
20 minutes + 2 ½ hours resting/proving

COOKING TIME
10 minutes

MAKES
8 flatbreads

- 2 cups (9 oz/250 g) whole wheat bread (strong wholemeal) flour
- 2 cups (9 oz/250 g) white bread (strong white) flour, plus extra for dusting
- 2 ½ teaspoons active dry (fast-action) yeast
- 1 teaspoon salt

See pages 190–191 for image

Growing up in Lebanon, I'd eat manoushe for breakfast, golden flatbreads often topped with za'atar made from thyme leaves that had been laid out to dry in the sunshine. We'd go round to the house where my mother baked her bread and, as it came out of the oven, we'd drizzle on a little olive oil and salt, and eat it right there and then. In London I haven't found anywhere that makes them like my mum used to, so I bake my own. In my last book I suggested topping simply with a za'atar blend and oil, in a traditional way, but I've included another few favorite toppings below. The parsley butter makes a great addition to a mezze spread, whilst the other two are morning choices in my house.

PREPARATION

In a large mixing bowl, combine the flours, yeast, and salt. Slowly add 1 cup (8 fl oz/250 ml) lukewarm water, mixing with a wooden spoon until a dough forms. You may need to add a little more water to bring the dough together.

Knead for a few minutes on an oiled work surface until the dough starts to become a little more elastic. Put the dough into a lightly oiled bowl, cover with a dish towel, and let rise in a warm place for about 2 hours, or until doubled in size.

Knead again and divide into 4 equal portions. Put each piece of dough into a separate oiled bowl and let rise again for 30 minutes.

Preheat the oven to 400°F/200°C/Gas Mark 6.

Divide each ball in half and roll into circles about 4 ½–5 ½ inches/12–14 cm in diameter and ¼ inch/5 mm thick

Add the topping of your choice (see pages 189–192), then place the flatbreads on wax (greaseproof) paper-lined baking sheets and bake for 10 minutes, or until lightly risen and golden brown with a crisp base. Serve warm.

Swiss Chard and Nutmeg

PREPARATION TIME
10 minutes

COOKING TIME
—

MAKES
topping for 8 flatbreads

1–2 tablespoons olive oil
2 garlic cloves, finely chopped
4 generous handfuls of Swiss chard (about 5 oz/150 g), stripped from the stalks and coarsely chopped (save the stalks to cook a vegetable accompaniment, rather than wasting them)
½ teaspoon freshly grated nutmeg
pinch of sea salt

See pages 190–191 for image

PREPARATION
Warm the olive oil in a skillet or frying pan over medium heat, then cook the garlic for 1–2 minutes until starting to turn golden. Add the chard, nutmeg, and salt and cook for 5 minutes, until the chard has wilted. Set aside to cool.

Squeeze out any excess moisture through a strainer (sieve) before topping your manoushe.

Orange-Blossom Labneh with Honey and Pistachios

PREPARATION TIME
5 minutes

COOKING TIME
—

MAKES
topping for 8 flatbreads

2 tablespoons Labneh (see page 10)
½ teaspoon orange blossom water
handful of shelled pistachios (1–1 ½ oz/30–40 g), coarsely chopped
squeeze of honey, per manoushe

See pages 190–191 for image

PREPARATION
Mix the labneh and orange blossom water and spread this over the manoushe, then sprinkle with the nuts and drizzle with honey.

1. Chickpea Savory Pancake with Za'atar (p.193)

Manoushe: 2. Lemon Parsley Butter (p.192) 3. Orange-Blossom Labneh with Honey and Pistachios (p.189) 4. Swiss Chard and Nutmeg (p.189)

Lemon Parsley Butter

PREPARATION TIME
5 minutes

COOKING TIME
–

MAKES
topping for 8 flatbreads

2 tablespoons (1 oz/25 g) butter, softened
handful of parsley, coarsely chopped
zest of ½ lemon
salt and pepper

See pages 190–191 for image

PREPARATION
Place the softened butter in a small bowl and stir in the parsley and lemon zest. Season with salt and pepper to taste.

Chickpea Savory Pancake with Za'atar

PREPARATION TIME
5 minutes + 30 minutes resting

COOKING TIME
10 minutes

SERVES
2–4 as a starter or snack
(makes 2 large pancakes)

1 cup (4 oz/120 g) chickpea (gram/besan) flour
¼ teaspoon sea salt
1 tablespoon extra virgin olive oil, plus 1 tablespoon to drizzle
2 teaspoons Za'atar (see page 13)
olive oil, for frying

TO SERVE (OPTIONAL)

Pink Pickled Turnips (see page 16)
bitter salad leaves
parsley leaves

See pages 190–191 for image

A lot of cultures have some version of a flatbread or pancake made with chickpea (gram) flour. Topped with traditional Lebanese Pink Pickled Turnips (see page 16), za'atar, and plenty of fresh parsley, my version is a perfect snack or light lunch.

PREPARATION

Put the flour and salt in a mixing bowl, then gradually whisk in 1 ¼ cups (10 fl oz/300 ml) lukewarm water and extra virgin olive oil until there are no lumps. Let the batter rest for 30 minutes.

Meanwhile preheat the broiler (grill) to high.

When ready to cook, swirl a little olive oil into an 11-inch/28-cm skillet or frying pan over medium-high heat. When hot, pour in half the batter to cover the bottom of the pan, and cook for 2–3 minutes, until you see bubbles starting to form in the center. Place under the broiler for 3–4 minutes to cook the top of the pancake. Keep warm in a low oven while you cook the other pancake.

Repeat with the second half of the batter.

Sprinkle with za'atar and drizzle over some extra virgin olive oil to finish. Serve immediately, with pickled turnips, bitter salad leaves, and fresh parsley.

Sweet Blessed Buns

PREPARATION TIME	COOKING TIME	SERVES
30 minutes + 2 hours proving	20–25 minutes	12 buns

½ cup (4 fl oz/120 ml) whole milk, plus extra for glazing
7 tablespoons (3 ½ oz/100 g) butter
3 ⅔ cups (1 lb 2 oz/500 g) white bread (strong white) flour
2 ½ teaspoons active dry (fast-action) yeast
½ cup (3 ½ oz/100 g) superfine (caster) sugar
pinch of salt
1 teaspoon cardamom seeds, ground in a pestle and mortar

Pillowy and fragrant with cardamom, these rolls look so pretty fresh out of the oven. Here in London, I often make them around Easter time but really they are delicious all year round.

These buns are distributed in church, but are also sold in stores and often baked at home for the priest, if he visits. I've added a bit of cardamom to this recipe, which isn't strictly traditional but adds an extra dimension of warmth that is so welcome in a colder climate.

PREPARATION

In a small saucepan, warm the milk and butter together with ½ cup (4 fl oz/120 ml) water over medium-low heat, until the butter melts.

Sift the flour into a large mixing bowl and stir in the yeast, sugar, salt, and ground cardamom. Make a well in the middle and pour in the warm liquid. Mix with a wooden spoon to form a dough. If it looks too sticky or too dry, add a little flour or water (use your judgment—you are looking for a dough that comes together in a ball and isn't too scrappy or wet).

Use your hands to bring the dough together in a ball, then turn out onto a lightly floured surface and knead for at least 10 minutes, until smooth and elastic. To test this, pinch a tennis-ball sized amount together between your finger and thumb, and poke with the forefinger of your other hand. If the indent bounces back, your dough is in good shape.

Form the dough into a ball and place in a lightly floured bowl. Cover the bowl with plastic wrap (clingfilm) and let rise in a warm place for at least 1 hour, until doubled in size.

Line a large baking sheet with parchment (baking) paper. Uncover the dough, knock it back by punching it down a few times, and knead for another few minutes. Shape the dough into 12 small rolls, place on the lined baking sheet, cover with a clean dish towel and let rise for another hour or so, until puffed up and increased in size again.

Preheat the oven to 400°F/200°C/Gas Mark 6.

Brush each roll with milk to glaze and bake in the center of the oven for 20 minutes, until deep golden on top and hollow-sounding when you tap the bottoms. Transfer to a wire rack to cool. Serve with butter.

Bulgur Wheat Bread with Za'atar

PREPARATION TIME
20 minutes + 2 hours rising

COOKING TIME
20–25 minutes

MAKES
3 flatbreads

⅓ cup (3 oz/80 g) cooked bulgur wheat, well drained
scant 1 cup (4 oz/120 g) whole wheat (wholemeal) flour, plus extra for dusting
¾ cup plus 2 tablespoons (4 oz/120 g) white bread (strong white) flour
½ teaspoon salt
1 x ¼-oz/7-g sachet active dry (fast-action) yeast
3 tablespoons olive oil, plus extra for greasing
1 tablespoon Za'atar (see page 13)

This is a version of a recipe that has been in my family for many years. It uses typical Lebanese ingredients, incorporating cooked bulgur for texture and moisture, and finishing with the heady blend of za'atar that we Lebanese love to sprinkle on most things!

These flatbreads are ideal served with the Crispy Artichoke Hearts with Za'atar Aioli (see page 48).

PREPARATION
Combine the cooked bulgur wheat, flours, salt, and yeast in a large bowl. Add enough warm water to form a wet dough, around ¾ cup (6 fl oz/175 ml).

Turn out onto a floured work surface and knead for about 10 minutes, until smooth and elastic. (Alternatively, this will take about 5 minutes in an electric mixer with a dough hook attachment.) Shape the dough into a ball, then put into a well-oiled mixing bowl and cover with plastic wrap (clingfilm) or a damp towel. Let rise in a warm place for 1 hour, or until doubled in size.

Grease 3 large roasting pans or baking pans, about 8 x 12 inches (20 x 30 cm).

Knock back the dough, then divide into 3 equal portions. Roll and stretch each portion to a rectangle shape just big enough to fit inside the greased pans. Push down into the dough with your fingers, almost to the bottom, to make deep dimples across the surface. Brush each flatbread with oil and sprinkle with za'atar, then cover and let rest for 1 hour.

Preheat the oven to 425°F/220°C/Gas Mark 7.

Bake in the center of the oven one at a time for 20–25 minutes until deep golden. Serve warm.

Halloumi-Stuffed Loaf

PREPARATION TIME
30 minutes + 2 hours rising

COOKING TIME
30 minutes

SERVES
6–8

- 3 x ¼-oz/7-g sachets active dry (fast-action) yeast
- 4 ½ cups (1 lb 5 oz/600 g) all-purpose (plain) flour, plus extra for dusting
- 3 teaspoons sea salt
- 1 tablespoon olive oil, plus extra for greasing
- 9 oz/250 g halloumi, drained and diced into ¼-inch/5-mm cubes
- zest of 1 lemon
- 1 ½ teaspoons dried mint

Adding grated halloumi to this bread takes it to another level of delicious. A real family favorite whenever I make it.

PREPARATION

Measure out 1 ⅔ cups (14 fl oz/400 ml) lukewarm water.

Place the yeast with scant ½ cup (3 ½ fl oz/100ml) of the water into a small bowl. Stir to dissolve and let sit for 5–10 minutes, until the mixture bubbles.

Sift together the flour and salt, then gradually add the yeast mixture, oil, and the remaining water to make a soft, sticky dough. Knead for 10 minutes—it will be quite a wet dough. Transfer to an oiled bowl, cover with a clean dish towel and let rise for 1 hour.

Meanwhile, mix the halloumi, lemon zest, and dried mint together in a medium bowl.

Lightly grease a deep roasting pan.

Knock back the dough and divide into 2 balls. Roll out one ball into a rough rectangle, about 12 x 8 inches/30 x 20 cm, or to fit the base of your pan. Press into the bottom of the roasting pan. Sprinkle over the halloumi mixture, leaving a ½-inch/1-cm border at the sides. Roll out the other ball of dough to a similar-sized rectangle and place on top, pinching the sides together to fully encase the filling. Let rise again for 1 hour, covered with plastic wrap (clingfilm) this time.

Preheat the oven to 475°F/240°C/Gas Mark 9.

Once risen, push down into the dough with your fingers, almost to the bottom, to make deep dimples across the surface. Bake in the hot oven for 10 minutes, then turn the heat down to 400°F/200°C/Gas Mark 6 and bake for a further 20 minutes. The loaf should sound hollow when tapped, if not return to the oven for a further 5 minutes. Turn out of the pan and cool on a wire rack.

Pita Bread

PREPARATION TIME	COOKING TIME	MAKES
25 minutes + 1 hour rising	10 minutes	6

2 ½ teaspoons active dry (fast-action) yeast
1 tablespoon honey or superfine (caster) sugar
3¼ cups (1 lb/450 g) white bread (strong white) flour, plus extra for dusting
1½ teaspoons sea salt
scant ½ cup (3 ½ fl oz/100 ml) warm milk
vegetable oil, for greasing

This (almost) flatbread is loved around the world. It famously puffs up and then sinks, leaving a hollow "pocket" perfect for all sorts of fillings. It's also great for dipping and can be toasted and used in salads, too.

PREPARATION

Measure out ⅔ cup (5 fl oz/150 ml) lukewarm water. Spoon 3 tablespoons of the water into a small bowl and stir in the yeast to dissolve. Stir in the honey or sugar.

Sift together the flour and salt into a large mixing bowl and stir in the yeast mixture.

Gradually add the remaining water and milk, mixing with a wooden spoon until a dough forms.

Turn out onto a floured work surface and knead for about 10 minutes, until smooth and elastic. Shape the dough into a ball, then put it into a bowl, cover with oiled plastic wrap (clingfilm), and let rise for 1 hour, or until doubled in size.

Preheat the oven to 450°F/230°C/Gas Mark 8.

Divide the dough into 6 equal pieces and roll each one out on a floured work surface to an 8-inch (20-cm) circle. Lift onto baking sheets and bake for 7–9 minutes, or until risen and golden.

These pitas are best served warm.

Cumin Seed Crackers

PREPARATION TIME
20 minutes + 30 minutes cooling

COOKING TIME
25–30 minutes

MAKES
about 24 crackers

3 tablespoons olive oil, plus extra for brushing
scant 2 cups (9 oz/250 g) all-purpose (plain) flour
6 tablespoons (2 oz/50 g) buckwheat flour
½ teaspoon chili flakes
1 teaspoon cumin seeds, plus a pinch for sprinkling
flaky sea salt

See pages 204–205 for image

These represent everything I like in a cracker; they are thin, flavorsome, and so light I can enjoy three or more at a time. Just like the crackers opposite, they keep well and the dough is easily frozen.

PREPARATION
Preheat the oven to 350°F/180°C/Gas Mark 4.

In a large mixing bowl, mix the olive oil, flours, spices, and a pinch of sea salt, until evenly combined. Make a well in the center and slowly pour in ⅔ cup (5 fl oz/150 ml) of cold water, mixing all the time with a wooden spoon, until a dough forms.

Lay a large sheet of parchment (baking) paper on your work surface and brush with olive oil. Transfer the dough to the sheet and cover with another sheet of parchment paper. Roll the dough out between the sheets as thinly as you can, ideally to ¹⁄₁₆–⅛-inch (2–3 mm) thick. Remove the top sheet of parchment paper and use the bottom sheet to transfer the rolled dough to a large baking sheet. Sprinkle over the reserved cumin seeds and a pinch of sea salt.

Bake for 25–30 minutes, until deep golden all over.

Let the cooked sheet cool on a wire rack for about 30 minutes, or until completely cool, then break into irregular shard-like pieces. Serve with Classic Hummus (see page 45) or Babaganoush (see page 32).

Chickpea and Za'atar Crackers

PREPARATION TIME
30 minutes + 30 minutes chilling

COOKING TIME
25 minutes

MAKES
about 24 crackers

2 generous cups (10 oz/275 g) chickpea (gram/besan) flour, plus extra for dusting
1 teaspoon baking powder
3 tablespoons olive oil, plus extra for drizzling
½ teaspoon salt
1 tablespoon Za'atar (see page 13)

See pages 204–205 for image

These crackers are lovely with any kind of dip. I like to make two batches of these at times of celebration or when I'm having guests for a few days; they keep well in a sealed container for 5 days or more. For smaller gatherings, consider freezing half of the dough for another time.

PREPARATION

In a large bowl, mix the chickpea (gram/besan) flour and baking powder together until no lumps are visible. Add the olive oil and mix through with a fork. Slowly pour in scant ½ cup (3½ fl oz/100 ml) of warm water, then add the salt, continuing to mix with the fork until the mixture comes together as a dough. Be careful not to over-mix; you don't want a sticky mass, as it will become difficult to work with. If this does happen, add a little more chickpea flour.

Dust a clean work surface with chickpea flour and turn out the dough onto it. Knead for 5 minutes, until the dough feels smooth (it won't feel elastic like bread dough), then divide into two balls, cover with plastic wrap (clingfilm) and chill well in the refrigerator for at least 30 minutes.

Preheat the oven to 350°F/180°C/Gas Mark 4. Line a large baking sheet with parchment (baking) paper.

Roll out each ball of chilled dough between two sheets of oiled parchment paper, to an even thickness of about ⅛ inch (3–4 mm). Use a sharp knife to cut the dough into shapes (personally, I prefer triangles), then carefully lift the cut pieces onto the lined baking sheet. Sprinkle with za'atar, drizzle with olive oil, and bake for 25 minutes, until golden.

Transfer the cooked crackers onto a wire rack to cool completely.

1. Cumin Seed Crackers (p.202) 2. Smoky Eggplant and Cilantro Tartlets (p.207) 3. Fava Bean and Artichoke Tartlets (p.206) 4. Chickpea and Za'atar Crackers (p.203)

Fava Bean and Artichoke Tartlets

PREPARATION TIME
25 minutes + 20 minutes chilling + 10 minutes cooling

COOKING TIME
25 minutes

MAKES
6–8 tartlets

- ⅔ cup (3 ½ oz/100 g) frozen fava (broad) beans
- 1 (11 ½-oz/320-g) sheet ready-rolled puff pastry
- 12 sprigs of mint (reserve a few smaller leaves for garnish)
- salt and pepper
- 1 tablespoon thick Greek yogurt
- 1 egg, beaten
- 6–8 preserved artichoke hearts (from a jar)
- 2 scallions (spring onions), thinly sliced at an angle
- 1 lemon, cut into wedges, to serve

See pages 204–205 for image

Irresistible spring tartlets filled with fava (broad) beans and artichokes. Perfect party food to enjoy with a glass of something sparkling.

PREPARATION

Put the fava (broad) beans into a bowl and pour over boiling water to cover. Set aside for 3-4 minutes.

Meanwhile, line a baking sheet with parchment (baking) paper. Roll the pastry out to a thickness of ¼ inch (4–5 mm). Cut 6–8 rings of pastry, using a 4-inch (10-cm) pastry cutter. Use a smaller pastry cutter or a sharp knife to mark out a smaller circle in the center, then use a spatula to lift the whole circles onto the baking sheet. Chill in the refrigerator for 20 minutes.

Preheat the oven to 350°F/180°C/Gas Mark 4.

Pop the soaked fava beans from their shells and discard the lighter green skins. Set a small handful of the beans aside and put the rest into a bowl. Add the chopped mint leaves and Greek yogurt, then lightly mash with a fork or potato masher, until the beans are broken up, but still have some texture. Taste, then season with salt and pepper to taste.

Prick the chilled pastry rounds with a fork. Brush the with beaten egg, then bake for 20 minutes until golden and puffed up. Let cool for 10 minutes.

Meanwhile, heat a ridged grill (griddle) pan over very high heat. Grill the artichoke hearts for about 3 minutes, turning them until well charred on all sides.

Push down on the middle of each baked pastry round to form a central cavity, then fill each with the fava bean mixture, dividing it equally among the tartlets. Top with the reserved beans, charred artichokes, reserved mint leaves, and scallions (spring onions).

Serve with lemon wedges on the side.

Smoky Eggplant and Cilantro Tartlets

PREPARATION TIME
25 minutes + 20 minutes chilling + 20 minutes cooling

COOKING TIME
30–35 minutes (if grilling directly over gas flame)

MAKES
8 tartlets

1 large eggplant (aubergine)
1 (11 ½-oz/320-g) sheet ready-rolled puff pastry
1 garlic clove, coarsely chopped
1 small bunch cilantro (coriander)
zest and juice of ½ lemon, or more to taste
2 tablespoons extra virgin olive oil, or more to taste
4 tablespoons thick Greek yogurt, soft goat's curd, or goat's cheese
1 egg, beaten
2 tablespoons pomegranate seeds
salt and pepper

See pages 204–205 for image

Another version of party-perfect tarts with a late-summer filling of spiced eggplant (aubergine), cilantro (coriander) and goat's curd. If you can't find goat's curd, a mild goat's cheese will do the trick.

PREPARATION
Preheat the broiler (grill) to its highest setting.

Grill the eggplant (aubergine) for 20-25 minutes, turning regularly, until the skin is blackened and bubbling (the skin may split, but that's fine). Alternatively, push a metal fork or skewer into the stem of the eggplant and char directly over a high gas flame for 12 minutes, turning regularly. Once the eggplant is softened and the skin is blackened and charred all over, set aside until cool enough to handle.

Meanwhile, line a baking sheet with parchment (baking) paper. Roll the pastry out to a thickness of ¼ inch (4–5 mm). Cut 6–8 rings of pastry, using a 4-inch (10-cm) pastry cutter. Use a smaller pastry cutter or a sharp knife to mark out a smaller circle in the center, then use a spatula to lift the whole circles onto the baking sheet. Chill in the refrigerator for 20 minutes.

When the eggplant is cool enough to handle, chop off the stem-end, peel away the skin, and coarsely chop the flesh. Put the flesh into a colander in the sink for the bitter juices to drain away.

Preheat the oven to 350°F/180°C/Gas Mark 4.

Put the drained eggplant into a food processor with the garlic, most of the cilantro (coriander) leaves and stalks (reserve a few sprigs for garnish), lemon zest and juice, and olive oil. Blend on high speed until well combined (about 45 seconds). With the motor still running, add 1 tablespoon of yogurt or goat's curd, and 1 tablespoon of cold water. Transfer the mixture into a mixing bowl and add salt, pepper, extra lemon juice, or extra olive oil, to taste.

Brush the chilled pastry rounds with beaten egg, and prick the inner circles with a fork a few times. Bake for 20 minutes until golden and puffed up. Let cool for 10 minutes.

When cool, push down on the middle of each baked pastry round to form a central cavity. Fill each cavity with eggplant mixture and top with a dollop of the yogurt or goat's curd. Sprinkle over the reserved cilantro leaves and a few pomegranate seeds.

Serve warm or at room temperature. Any leftover eggplant mixture can be spooned through Classic Hummus (see page 45) or onto toasted flatbreads.

Kale and Chile Rolls

PREPARATION TIME
25 minutes

COOKING TIME
23 minutes

MAKES
18 rolls

3 oz/80 g curly kale, shredded
3 oz/80 g feta cheese or goat's curd, crumbled
1 red chile, finely chopped
1 small bunch parsley, finely chopped
3 sheets phyllo (filo) pastry (covered with a damp cloth to prevent them from drying)
7 tablespoons (3 ½ oz/100 g) unsalted butter, melted
1 tablespoon Za'atar (see page 13)
salt and pepper

I love experimenting with flavors and shapes when cooking with phyllo (filo) pastry. These cigar-shaped rolls are probably the simplest pastries to make and yet are the most impressive. There is something about the pastry, crisped by butter and generously filled with salted cheese, that really lifts the spirit. They also freeze well, so I usually make two batches and keep a batch in the freezer. You can cook straight from frozen—add another 5 or 10 minutes to the cooking time and keep an eye on them.

PREPARATION
Bring a saucepan of well-salted water to a rolling boil. When this point is reached, plunge the kale into the saucepan and boil for 3 minutes, until softened and bright green. Drain in a colander under cold running water. When cool enough to handle, squeeze out as much water as possible, then put the kale into a mixing bowl with the cheese, chile, parsley, and a generous pinch of salt and pepper. Mix until well combined.

Preheat the oven to 350°F/180°C/Gas Mark 4. Line a baking sheet with parchment (baking) paper.

Lay the phyllo (filo) sheets on a work surface, covered with a damp cloth to prevent them from drying, and set the melted butter nearby. Cut each sheet into thirds lengthwise, then cut each piece in half widthwise. You should have 18 pieces of phyllo pastry. Keep them covered with the damp cloth while you work.

Take one piece of pastry and brush with melted butter. Arrange 1 teaspoon of the kale mixture in a thin log along one short end of the pastry, leaving ½ inch (1 cm) of pastry clear at each edge. Roll into a thin cigar shape, until you have about ½ inch (1 cm) of pastry left at the end, then tuck it in at both of the open sides to seal. Brush with melted butter and place on the lined baking sheet.

Repeat with the remaining phyllo sheets.

Sprinkle the cigars with the za'atar and bake in the oven for 20 minutes, until golden. Cool slightly before serving.

Spinach and Walnut Tartlets

PREPARATION TIME
15 minutes + cooling time

COOKING TIME
40–45 minutes

MAKES
12 tartlets

6 tablespoons butter
3 tablespoons olive oil
1 onion, sliced
1 teaspoon brown sugar
1 lb 8 ½ oz/700 g baby spinach
¼ teaspoon grated nutmeg
1 teaspoon Lebanese 7-Spice Seasoning (see page 12)
½ teaspoon salt
½ teaspoon pepper
9 oz/250 g phyllo (filo) pastry sheets (6–9 sheets, depending on brand, covered with a damp cloth to prevent them from drying)
1 ¼ cups (10 ½ fl oz/300 ml) heavy (double) cream
4 eggs, lightly beaten
⅓ cup (2 oz/50 g) shelled walnuts, roughly chopped
1 teaspoon honey
½ teaspoon ground turmeric

These are delicious little tarts to feed a crowd and have the appearance of something rather fiddly and sophisticated to put together, but are in fact very straightforward.

I adore this combination of warming spices with the spinach, which tempers the strong iron flavor of spinach when cooked.

Serve these tarts alongside some Turmeric Pickled Cauliflower (see page 18) and a couple of salads, or on trays at a drinks gathering.

PREPARATION

Heat 1 tablespoon of butter with 2 tablespoons of oil in a large saucepan over low heat until melted. Add the onion and sugar and cook for 20 minutes, stirring occasionally, until caramelized. Remove from the heat and set aside.

Heat the remaining tablespoon of oil in a large skillet or frying pan, add the spinach and cook until wilted, then stir in 1 tablespoon of butter. Put the spinach into a colander and squeeze out the excess liquid, then chop and put into a mixing bowl. Add the nutmeg, spice, salt, and pepper, mix well and set aside.

Preheat the oven to 350°F/180°C/Gas Mark 4.

Melt the remaining butter and put into a small bowl. Use a little of the butter to grease a 12-hole muffin pan.

Put the phyllo (filo) pastry sheets onto a clean surface, cut each sheet into 8 equal pieces (these will be squares or rectangles, depending on brand of pastry), then stack them up and cover with a damp cloth to prevent them drying out. Working one at a time, brush each piece of pastry with melted butter and lay in the prepared muffin pan, repeating until there are 4–6 layers of pastry sheets in each cup. Arrange the sheets so that each piece is rotated slightly, to give pretty rough edges. Brush the top layers with a little melted butter.

Spoon the spinach filling into each pastry case. Pour the cream into a small bowl, stir in the eggs, and season with salt and pepper. Pour a little of this mixture into each pastry case, then bake in the oven for 15–20 minutes, until the filling is set and the pastry is golden brown. Remove from the oven and let cool.

Meanwhile, toast the walnuts in a dry skillet or frying pan, then stir in the honey and turmeric. Remove from the heat and set aside in a warm place until ready to serve.

Serve the tarts topped with the caramelized onions and walnuts.

Chicken Fatteh

PREPARATION TIME	COOKING TIME	SERVES
20 minutes	50–55 minutes	4

1 cinnamon stick
6 cardamom seeds
4 cloves
3 skinless, boneless chicken breasts
1 tablespoon olive oil
1 onion, sliced
2 garlic cloves, crushed
1 teaspoon paprika
¾ cup (3 oz/80 g) pine nuts, toasted
2 Pita Breads (see page 200), toasted
salt and pepper

FOR THE YOGURT SAUCE
1 cup (8 fl oz/250 ml) plain (natural) yogurt
2 garlic cloves, crushed
2 tablespoons chopped mint
2 tarragon sprigs, chopped

Fatteh is served around Lebanon where I grew up in various guises but the most classic and recognized version is this one with shredded chicken and crispy pieces of pita bread, layered with spices and yogurt sauce.

This chicken fatteh is best assembled at the last minute, as people are gathering at the table, so get everything ready beforehand. If the fatteh sits for too long, the bread will turn from crispy to soggy and one of the best things about this dish is the delightful textures and flavors when it's enjoyed as soon as it's ready.

PREPARATION
Bring a pan of water to a boil and add the cinnamon stick, cardamom seeds, and cloves. Reduce the heat so that the surface of the water is barely bubbling, add the chicken, and poach for 45 minutes or until very tender. Lift out the chicken with a slotted spoon and let cool, then shred into bite-size pieces.

Heat the oil in a skillet or frying pan, add the onion, and cook over low heat, stirring occasionally, for 5 minutes until softened. Add the garlic and cook for another minute, then stir in the shredded chicken and paprika and season well with salt and pepper. Cook for a few minutes until heated through, then transfer to a warm serving dish.

Mix together all the ingredients for the yogurt sauce and spoon it over the chicken. Sprinkle with the pine nuts. Cut the toasted pita breads into squares, put them on top of the dish, and serve immediately.

Lamb Manakish

PREPARATION TIME
30 minutes + resting time

COOKING TIME
30–35 minutes

MAKES
2 large pizzas

1 ¾ cups (7 oz/200 g) hard (strong) whole wheat (wholemeal) bread flour
1 ⅓ cups (6 oz/175 g) all-purpose (plain) flour, plus extra for dusting
½ envelope active dry (fast-action) yeast
½ tablespoon salt
2 teaspoons extra virgin olive oil, plus extra for brushing
1 ¼ cups (½ pint/300 ml) lukewarm water

FOR THE TOPPING
14 oz/400 g ground (minced) lamb
2 garlic cloves, crushed
1 teaspoon dried mint
1 teaspoon ground cumin
1 teaspoon Lebanese 7-Spice Seasoning (see page 12)
4 tablespoons tomato paste (purée)
1 red onion, sliced
3 oz/85 g spicy sausage, sliced
2 tablespoons chopped mint
salt and pepper

Growing up in Lebanon, I remember the local women sharing the communal oven to bake dough for their family's bread needs for the day, and the smaller pieces of dough would be rolled and topped for breakfast (rolling them thinly would help them to cook quickly in the oven).

I like to serve this Lamb Manakish with the Pink Pickled Turnips (see page 16) and some minty yogurt on the side.

PREPARATION
First, make the dough. Mix together both types of flour, the yeast, and salt in a bowl, then add the oil and gradually stir in the lukewarm water until a dough forms. You may need a little less or more water to bring the dough together. Knead the dough for 10 minutes, then shape it into a ball, return it to the bowl, and dust with a little flour. Cover tightly with plastic wrap (clingfilm) and leave for 1 hour in a warm, dark place to rise.

Meanwhile, make the topping. Heat a heavy pan, add the lamb, and cook over medium heat, stirring frequently, for 8–10 minutes until evenly browned. Reduce the heat, add the garlic, mint, spices, and scant ½ cup (3½ fl oz/100 ml) water, and simmer, stirring occasionally, for 20 minutes. Remove from the heat and season well with salt and pepper.

Preheat the oven to 450°F/230°C/Gas Mark 8. Brush 2 baking sheets with oil.

Turn out the dough onto a lightly floured surface and punch down (knock back), then divide it in half with your hands. Roll out each piece of dough on a lightly floured surface to a circle and then place on the prepared baking sheets. Spread the tomato paste (purée) evenly over both dough bases. Divide the lamb mixture between them and spread to the edges of the dough. Top with the onion and sausage and bake for 10–15 minutes or until the bases are crispy.

Remove the pizzas from the oven, season with salt and pepper, and sprinkle with chopped mint. Cut the pizzas into slices and serve immediately.

Fish Shawarma

PREPARATION TIME	COOKING TIME	SERVES
15 minutes	12 minutes	2

14 oz/400 g cod loin
2 tablespoons olive oil
½ teaspoon sea salt
½ teaspoon pepper
pinch of paprika
1 tablespoon salted capers, rinsed
¼ iceberg lettuce, shredded
1 tablespoon chopped parsley
1 tablespoon chopped dill
1 tablespoon snipped chopped chives
8 cherry tomatoes, halved
2 Lebanese flatbreads, warmed in the oven or under the broiler (grill) for a few minutes
juice of ½ lemon
2 tablespoons Garlic Dip (see page 148)
salt and pepper

Shawarma is a cousin of the doner kebab, and is prepared by grilling meat or fish, and serving it in flatbreads with salad and tahini or garlic sauce. Some shawarma recipes require you to turn the meat on a spit for as long as a day, before slicing thinly, but this is my home-cooked version with flaky cod, fresh herb salad, and a punchy garlic sauce.

This is what I want to eat after a busy day out with family in the summer, collapsing around the table in the garden as we enjoy the last of the evening sun.

PREPARATION

Rub the cod loin with the olive oil, sea salt, ½ teaspoon pepper, and the paprika. Heat a skillet or frying pan, add the cod and capers, and cook for 5–6 minutes on each side or until the flesh flakes easily. Remove the pan from the heat, lift out the cod with a slotted spatula (fish slice), and flake the flesh into large pieces. Set aside with the capers and pan juices.

Put the lettuce, parsley, dill, chives, and tomatoes into a bowl and season with salt and black pepper. Lay out the flatbreads on a work surface and divide the salad between them. Top with the fish, capers, and a spoonful of garlic dip on each. Squeeze the lemon juice over the top and roll up tightly. Serve immediately.

CHAPTER EIGHT

Sweets

Beet and Chocolate Mousse Cakes

PREPARATION TIME
35 minutes

COOKING TIME
30–35 minutes

SERVES
6

7 oz/200 g cooked beets (beetroot)
7 oz/200 g semisweet (dark) chocolate
7 tablespoons (3 ½ oz/100 g) unsalted butter, diced, plus extra for greasing
3 eggs, separated
½ cup (3 ½ oz/100 g) superfine (caster) sugar
4 tablespoons cocoa powder
zest of 1 orange
pinch of salt
thick Greek yogurt, to serve

This has to be one of my very favorite puddings, with beautiful velvety color from the beets (beetroot), richness from the chocolate, and the zesty flavor of orange lifting it to the next level.

PREPARATION
Grate the beets (beetroot) on the medium holes of a box grater. Place the grated beets in a strainer (sieve) set over the sink and push the beets down to remove as much moisture as possible. Leave to drain.

Put the chocolate and butter in a heatproof bowl and set over a saucepan of barely simmering water. Make sure the bottom of the bowl is not touching the water. Stir frequently until the chocolate is almost melted, then take the pan off the heat and continue to stir until the chocolate is completely melted (the rest will melt with the residual heat). Add the drained beets and set aside to cool.

In a large bowl, beat the egg whites and sugar with an electric handheld mixer until bright white, glossy, and forming stiff peaks. This should take about 5 minutes.

Grease 6 ramekins or a muffin pan with butter and dust over 3 tablespoons of cocoa powder.

Whisk the egg yolks into the chocolate mixture until combined, then fold (don't beat) a spoonful of the egg whites into the chocolate mixture until fully incorporated. Add the remaining egg whites to the chocolate and fold again until fully incorporated. Stir in 1 tablespoon of cocoa powder, the orange zest, and salt.

Preheat the oven to 350°F/180°C/Gas Mark 4.

Divide the cake batter between the prepared ramekins/muffin pan, then put the ramekins/muffin pan into a deep roasting pan. Pour freshly boiled water around the ramekins/muffin pan until it comes halfway up the sides.

Bake in the center of the oven for 30–35 minutes, until the cakes are cracked on top with a bit of wobble still in the centers.

Eat with teaspoons straight from the ramekins, or if you've used a muffin pan then use a pallet knife to loosen and gently turn them out. Serve with thick Greek yogurt.

Favorite Ma'mool Cookies

PREPARATION TIME
20 minutes + 3 hours/
overnight standing time

COOKING TIME
25–30 minutes

MAKES
12–18 cookies

FOR THE DOUGH
1 stick (4 oz/120 g) unsalted butter, melted
1 ⅓ cups (8 oz/225 g) coarse semolina
2 tablespoons sugar
1 teaspoon mahleb
¾ cup (3 ½ oz/100 g) all-purpose (plain) flour
½ teaspoon baking soda (bicarbonate of soda)
1 tablespoon orange blossom water
confectioners' (icing sugar), for dusting

FOR THE WALNUT FILLING
½ cup (2 oz/50 g) finely chopped walnuts
½ teaspoon sugar
1 teaspoon orange blossom water

FOR THE PISTACHIO FILLING
½ cup (2 oz/50 g) shelled pistachio nuts
½ teaspoon sugar
1 teaspoon orange blossom water

FOR THE DATE FILLING
⅓ cup (2 oz/50 g) pitted chopped dates
½ teaspoon sugar
1 teaspoon allspice

See pages 224–225 for image

I have been making these pretty cookies for more years than I can remember—at Christmas, I make batches to give as gifts, packaged in boxes and tied with bright ribbons. There's something about the texture of the semolina in the dough that makes them very moreish. You can often find the molds in Middle Eastern stores. They're not expensive and are lovely objects to keep.

PREPARATION
To make the dough, melt the butter in a large saucepan, then stir in the semolina, sugar, and mahleb. Push the mixture down into the pan, cover, and remove from the heat. Let stand for at least 3 hours, or overnight, at room temperature.

To make the walnut filling, put the ingredients into a blender or food processor and process to fine crumbs. Repeat for the pistachio filling, and then the date filling. Keep them separate.

Return the pan of semolina mixture to a low heat for a few minutes to loosen, then remove from the heat and transfer into a bowl. Add the flour, baking soda (bicarbonate of soda), orange blossom water, and 1 tablespoon of water. Knead the mixture in the bowl for 5–10 minutes, until a dough forms. Add another 2–3 tablespoons of water, if required.

Preheat the oven to 325°F/160°C/Gas Mark 3.

To make the ma'mool, take a handful of dough and dust with flour, then flatten into a patty. Put 1 teaspoon of filling in the center of the patty and then wrap the dough around the filling. Roll in flour, then press into a ma'mool mold. Tap the mold on the work surface to release the cookie and put it onto a baking sheet. If you don't have molds, use an individual jelly mold or cut a decorative shape with a ravioli cutter.

Repeat this filling and shaping until all the dough and filling mixtures have been used up. Any leftover filling can be frozen.

Bake for 25–30 minutes, until golden. Remove from the oven and transfer the cookies to a wire rack to cool completely. Dust with confectioners' (icing) sugar, and store in an airtight container.

Tahini Brownies

PREPARATION TIME
15 minutes + cooling time

COOKING TIME
30–40 minutes

MAKES
24 brownies

12 oz/350 g semisweet (dark) chocolate (70% cocoa solids), broken into chunks
1 ½ cups (12 oz/350 g) unsalted butter, plus extra for greasing
4 large eggs
1 ¾ cups (12 oz/350 g) superfine (caster) sugar
1 tablespoon vanilla paste
1 tablespoon cocoa powder
1 ⅓ cups (6 oz/175 g) all-purpose (plain) flour
½ cup (2 oz/50 g) shelled pistachios, coarsely chopped
8 teaspoons Tahini (see page 12)

See pages 224–225 for image

These are a great crowd-pleaser at parties so I'll often make a double batch and put candles in for birthdays. The pretty swirl of tahini makes them somehow feel celebratory.

PREPARATION

Preheat the oven to 350°F/180°C/Gas Mark 4. Grease and line an 8 x 12-inch/20 x 30 cm baking pan with parchment (baking) paper.

Put the chocolate and butter in a heatproof bowl and set over a saucepan of barely simmering water. Make sure the bottom of the bowl is not touching the water. Stir frequently until the chocolate is almost melted, then take the pan off the heat and continue to stir until the chocolate is completely melted (the rest will melt with the residual heat). Set aside to cool.

Use an electric whisk to whisk the eggs, sugar, and vanilla in a large mixing bowl until light and fluffy. Fold in the cocoa powder and flour until completely combined. Stir in the melted chocolate mixture, followed by the pistachios. Pour the mixture into the prepared pan, then dot teaspoonfuls of the tahini on top in random places. Drag a skewer through the tahini and batter to create an attractive swirl pattern.

Bake in the center of the oven for 30 minutes, until firm to the touch but still soft and gooey in the center. Remove from the oven and let cool in the pan—the brownies will continue to cook as they cool.

When completely cool, remove from the pan and cut into 24 x 2-inch/5-cm square brownies (4 rows of 6). Serve with a strong, bitter Arabic coffee.

1. Tahini Brownies (p.223) 2. Favorite Ma'mool Cookies (p.222) 3. Pistachio and Pomegranate Cake (p.227) 4. Orange Blossom Water and Saffron Tartlets (p.226)

Orange Blossom Water and Saffron Tartlets

PREPARATION TIME
1 hour + 30 minutes cooling

COOKING TIME
20–25 minutes

MAKES
24 tartlets

butter, softened, or a neutral oil, for greasing
2 tablespoons confectioners' (icing) sugar
1 tablespoon all-purpose (plain) flour
1 (11 ½-oz/320-g) sheet ready-rolled puff pastry
½ cup (3 ½ oz/100 g) superfine (caster) sugar
1 egg, plus 3 egg yolks
2 tablespoons cornstarch (cornflour)
zest of 1 orange (removed with a vegetable peeler)
2 generous cups (17 fl oz/500 ml) whole (full-fat) milk
1 tablespoon orange blossom water
1 teaspoon vanilla paste
pinch of saffron

See pages 224–225 for image

These cheerful tarts are actually a version of the egg custard pastries, Pasteis de Nata, a Portuguese delicacy famously made in Lisbon for several hundred years. Mine have a more Middle Eastern flavor, with sunny notes of saffron, orange, and orange blossom. Please believe me when I say they will disappear very quickly!

PREPARATION

Grease two 12-hole mini-muffin/cupcake pans with softened butter or a neutral oil.

Mix 1 tablespoon of the confectioners' (icing) sugar and the flour together in a bowl, then use it to lightly dust your work surface, reserving about 1 teaspoon. Unroll the puff pastry sheet, if necessary, then use the reserved sugar/flour mixture to dust the surface of the pastry. Tightly roll the pastry into a log from one shorter side to the other. Cut into 24 thin rounds, then use a rolling pin to roll each round to a ¼-inch (½-cm) thickness. Push the rolled pastry into the holes in the pans to line them. The pastry can rise above the edges of the pan, as it will shrink as it cooks. Chill in the refrigerator.

Meanwhile, in a large saucepan, mix the superfine (caster) sugar, egg, egg yolks, and cornstarch (cornflour), whisking to combine. Place over a low heat, add the orange zest, and pour in the milk. Heat, whisking continuously, until the mixture thickens, but do not boil. Remove from the heat and stir in the orange blossom water, vanilla paste, and saffron. Cover with plastic wrap (clingfilm) to prevent a skin forming on top of the custard and let cool for 30 minutes.

Preheat the oven to 350°F/180°C/Gas Mark 4.

Remove the orange peel from the custard, then evenly spoon the custard between the chilled pastry cases. Sift the remaining confectioners' (icing) sugar over the top. Bake for 20–25 minutes, until golden and bubbling on top.

Let the tarts cool in the pans for 10 minutes, before transferring them to a wire rack to cool completely. Store in an airtight container and eat within 3 days.

Pistachio and Pomegranate Cake

PREPARATION TIME
25 minutes

COOKING TIME
40 minutes

MAKES
1 small 1-lb (450-g) loaf cake

7 tablespoons (3 ½ oz/100 g) unsalted butter, softened, plus extra for greasing
½ cup (3 ½ oz/100 g) golden superfine (caster) sugar
2 large eggs, beaten
1 cup (3 ½ oz/100 g) pistachio kernels, blitzed to a powder
scant ⅔ cup (3 oz/80 g) all-purpose (plain) flour
2 tablespoons thick Greek yogurt
1 small carrot, grated (about 2 ½ oz/60 g)
1 teaspoon vanilla paste
seeds from ½ pomegranate (about 3 ½ oz/100 g)

FOR THE ICING
2 oz (50 g) thick Greek yogurt
1 tablespoon confectioners' (icing) sugar
zest of ½ orange
seeds from other ½ pomegranate (about 3 ½ oz/100 g)

See pages 224–225 for image

I use pistachios here, instead of ground almonds, for a Middle Eastern twist on frangipane. This makes a lovely loaf to serve with a cup of afternoon tea.

PREPARATION
Grease and line a 1-lb (450-g) loaf tin and preheat the oven to 375°F/190°C/Gas Mark 5.

Beat the butter and sugar together with an electric whisk until light and fluffy, then slowly beat in the beaten egg until fully incorporated. Fold in the pistachios, flour, yogurt, carrot and vanilla paste, then push the juice from the pomegranate seeds through a (strainer) sieve over the bowl and mix to combine.

Pour the cake batter into the loaf tin and even out the top with a rubber spatula. Place in the oven at 375°F/190°C/Gas Mark 5 for 10 minutes, then reduce the oven temperature to 300°F/150°C/Gas Mark 2 and cook for a further 30 minutes.

While the cake is cooking, beat the yogurt, confectioners' (icing) sugar, and orange zest together.

After the 30 minutes is up, test the cake is done by inserting a knife—if it comes out clean, remove the cake to the side to cool. If the knife doesn't come out clean, return the cake to the oven for another 3 minutes and test again.

After 10 minutes, remove the cake from the tin and place on a wire rack to cool. Once the cake is cool, spread the yogurt icing over the top and sprinkle with pomegranate seeds.

Baked Cardamom and Almond Milk Rice Pudding

PREPARATION TIME
20 minutes + 30 minutes infusing time

COOKING TIME
1 hour 10 minutes– 1 hour 25 minutes

SERVES
6

2 ½ cups (20 fl oz/600 ml) almond milk, sweetened or unsweetened, according to taste
1 teaspoon cardamom seeds (from about 15 pods), crushed in a pestle and mortar
scant ⅓ cup (1 oz/30 g) almond meal (ground almonds)
scant ½ cup (3 ¼ oz/90 g) pudding rice
1 teaspoon vanilla paste
generous ⅓ cup (3 oz/80 g) golden superfine (caster) sugar
Fig and Rose Jam (see page 28) or Stewed Plums with Orange (see page 244), to serve

I love to serve this rice pudding with Fig and Rose Jam (see page 28) or Stewed Plums with Orange (see page 244). Rice pudding is such a comforting dish, and the almond and cardamom make it both delicate and fragrant, too.

PREPARATION
Preheat the oven to 375°F/190°C/Gas Mark 5.

Put the almond milk and cardamom seeds in a saucepan and bring to the boil. Remove the pan from the heat and set aside to infuse for 30 minutes.

Spread the almond meal (ground almonds) in an even layer over a roasting pan and toast for 5 minutes in the oven, until starting to color. Remove from the oven.

Reduce the oven temperature to 300°F/150°C/Gas Mark 2.

Mix the pudding rice with the toasted almonds and divide between 6 ramekins (at least ⅔-cup/5-fl oz/150-ml capacity), leaving a generous amount of space at the top for the milk.

Transfer the infused milk to a measuring jug and stir in the vanilla and sugar until dissolved. Pour scant ½ cup (3 ½ fl oz/100 ml) into each ramekin.

Arrange the ramekins in a roasting pan and bake for 1 hour 10 minutes–1 hour 25 minutes or until the rice is tender and the puddings are golden.

Serve with either Fig and Rose Jam (see page 28) or Stewed Plums with Orange (see page 244).

Blood Orange and Pomegranate Sorbet

PREPARATION TIME
35 minutes + 5 hours
freezing time

COOKING TIME
—

MAKES
generous 2 cups
(17 fl oz/500 ml)

8 blood oranges
1 pomegranate, quartered and seeds removed
scant ⅔ cup (4 oz/120 g) superfine (caster) sugar
1 small thumb-sized piece fresh ginger, peeled and finely grated
juice of 1 lime

I love this zippy sorbet when blood oranges are in season in January. It is always a welcome antidote to the rich, warming food that I also crave when it's gray and cold outside.

PREPARATION

Wash 2 of the blood oranges well and finely grate the zest. Set the zest aside.

Halve all the blood oranges and squeeze the juice through a strainer (sieve) set over a large measuring cup (measuring jug) or bowl. The strainer should catch any pips. Next, place the pomegranate seeds in the strainer and use the back of a wooden spoon to press down and remove as much juice as possible. You need 1 ⅔ cups (14 fl oz/400 ml) of juice in total.

Pour scant ½ cup (3 ½ fl oz/ 100 ml) of the juice into a small saucepan, then add the sugar and ginger. Warm over medium heat until the sugar has dissolved. Remove from the heat and stir in the lime juice. Let cool for 10 minutes, then stir in the rest of the orange and pomegranate juices.

Pour the juice and the reserved orange zest into a strong freezerproof container with a lid and put into the freezer. Remove every 90 minutes to whisk vigorously with a fork, until a sorbet forms—this usually takes about 5 hours.

Apricots with Mascarpone

PREPARATION TIME
10 minutes + 10 minutes cooling

COOKING TIME
10 minutes

SERVES
4–6

6 apricots, halved and pitted
3 tablespoons granulated sugar
⅔ cup (5 oz/150 g) mascarpone cheese
1 tablespoon honey
1 teaspoon orange blossom water
1 ½ oz/40 g slivered (flaked) almonds or coarsely chopped pistachios
1 tablespoon coriander seeds, coarsely bashed in a pestle and mortar

The summery flavor of apricots goes so beautifully with delicate orange blossom and the creamy sweetness of mascarpone cheese. Serve with some Iced Cardamom Coffee (see page 256) for posh elevenses.

PREPARATION
Preheat the broiler (grill) to its highest setting.
   Arrange the apricots, cut side up, on a baking sheet and sprinkle the sugar over.
   Grill for 5–7 minutes, turning them a couple of times, until the cut sides are blistered and golden in places, like the top of a crème brûlée. Let cool for 10 minutes.
   Meanwhile, whisk the mascarpone with the honey and orange blossom water, until light and fluffy.
   Gently toast the chopped nuts and coriander seeds in a dry skillet or frying pan until golden and fragrant.
   Place a heaping spoonful of the mascarpone mixture in the middle of each hollow at the center of the apricots and sprinkle over the toasted nuts. Serve with Iced Cardamom Coffee (see page 256).

Arabic Coffee Mousse

PREPARATION TIME	COOKING TIME	SERVES
20 minutes + 3 hours chilling or overnight	–	6

6 tablespoons (3 fl oz/90 ml) espresso or strong coffee

seeds of 3 cardamom pods, crushed in a pestle and mortar

4 oz/120 g semisweet (dark) chocolate (at least 70% cocoa solids), broken into small pieces, plus extra to serve

2 large eggs, separated

2 tablespoons superfine (caster) sugar

A perfect grown-up dessert to make ahead before a dinner party. When I'm trying to impress, I like to fill little glasses with this coffee mousse and serve with the Rose and Cardamom Shortbread (see page 243).

PREPARATION

Place 6 glasses (at least ½–⅔-cup/3 ½–5-fl oz/100–150 ml capacity) in the refrigerator to chill.

Put the espresso, cardamom seeds, and chocolate pieces into a heatproof bowl and set over a saucepan of barely simmering water. Make sure the bottom of the bowl is not touching the water. Stir frequently until the chocolate is almost melted, then take the pan off the heat and continue to stir until the chocolate is completely melted (the rest will melt with the residual heat). Set aside to cool.

Using an electric whisk, whisk the egg whites in a bowl until soft peaks form, then add the sugar and whisk on high speed until the mixture is glossy and holds its shape when you lift up the whisk.

Rinse and dry the whisk attachments, then whisk the egg yolks into the cooled chocolate mixture until fully incorporated. Fold a spoonful of the egg whites into the chocolate mixture to loosen, then fold in the rest of the whites until no white streaks are visible.

Spoon the mousse evenly into the chilled glasses and chill in the refrigerator for at least 3 hours or overnight, until set. Grate more chocolate over the top just before serving.

Quinces Poached in Their Own Syrup

PREPARATION TIME
15 minutes

COOKING TIME
1 hour 40 minutes

SERVES
8

- juice of 1 lemon (keep the juiced halves)
- 4 quinces
- 8 cloves
- ¾ cup (5 oz/150 g) golden superfine (caster) sugar
- 7 oz/200 g clotted cream or heavy whipping cream, to serve
- ⅔ cup (2 oz/50 g) slivered (flaked) almonds, toasted, to serve

This dish takes a bit of time but is so worth the effort. The natural pectin in the quince peel and seeds thickens the poaching syrup, giving an indulgent, chewy, and candied texture. Serving the quince with clotted cream or heavy whipping cream gives a lovely contrast.

PREPARATION
Preheat the oven to 300°F/150°C/Gas Mark 2.

Fill a large bowl with water and add the lemon juice and the juiced lemon halves.

Peel and halve the quinces, then scoop out the core with a melon baller, putting each prepared quince half into the bowl with the lemons. Spread the quince peel and cores in an even layer in a small roasting pan, in which the quinces can fit snugly. Arrange the quinces, cut side up, in the pan.

Place 1 clove in each quince half, then sprinkle over the sugar and pour scant 1 cup (7 fl oz/200 ml) of water around them. Cover the pan with aluminum foil and bake for 40–60 minutes (depending on the size and ripeness of the quinces—large, under-ripe quinces will take longer). Remove the pan from the oven, remove and discard the foil, then turn the halves over and spoon over the syrup. Return to the oven for a further 40 minutes.

Serve warm with clotted cream or heavy whipping cream and a few slivered (flaked) almonds scattered over the top.

Walnut and Rose Baklava

PREPARATION TIME
30 minutes

COOKING TIME
45–50 minutes

MAKES
about 24 pieces

1 (9-oz/250-g) packet chilled (not frozen) phyllo (filo) pastry
1 ¾ sticks (7 oz/200 g) unsalted butter, melted

FOR THE FILLING
1 ½ cups (7 oz/200 g) blanched almonds
1 ¼ cups (5 oz/150 g) walnut pieces (break any whole ones)
½ teaspoon ground cinnamon
½ teaspoon allspice
2 tablespoons superfine (caster) sugar
2 tablespoons unsalted butter, melted

FOR THE SYRUP
generous ½ cup (5 oz/150 g) runny honey
½ cup (3 ½ oz/100 g) superfine (caster) sugar
zest and juice of 1 lemon
1 teaspoon rosewater

See pages 240–241 for image

A strong, bitter Arabic coffee and a sticky sweet diamond of baklava is one of life's simple pleasures. I've included three recipes here, because baklava is one of my favorite pastries. It's well worth making it yourself.

PREPARATION
First, make the filling. Process the almonds, walnuts, spices, and sugar in a food processor to coarse crumbs, then transfer to a mixing bowl and stir in the melted butter.

Unroll the chilled phyllo (filo) pastry sheets and cover with a damp cloth to prevent the sheets from drying out.

Preheat the oven to 325°F/160°C/Gas Mark 3.

Grease the bottom of a 8 x 12-inch (20 x 30-cm) roasting pan, then lay one of the shorter edges of the pastry along the long side of the roasting pan. Brush the pastry sheet with melted butter, then fold the sheet over on itself and brush the other side with butter as well. If your pan is the right size, you should be able to double up a sheet of pastry perfectly. Now, starting from the other long edge of the roasting pan, lay a second sheet of pastry and draw towards the other side of the roasting pan. Brush with butter, fold again, and brush again. You should have 4 layers of buttered pastry in the pan. Evenly spread a third of the filling over the pastry sheets, then lay another buttered sheet of pastry over the top. Continue with these steps until you have 3 layers of filling, then finish with another 4 layers of pastry. Generously butter the top layer.

Use a sharp knife to cut the baklava into 1 ¼-inch (3-cm) diamonds or squares. Bake in the center of the oven for 45–50 minutes or until golden, covering with aluminum foil after 30 minutes if the pastry is browning too quickly.

Next, make the syrup. Put the honey, sugar, and lemon juice in a small saucepan along with scant ½ cup (3 ½ fl oz/100 ml) water and warm over medium-low heat until the sugar has dissolved. Brush down the sides a few times with a wet pastry brush to get rid of any sugar crystals, as this may result in crystals forming in the baklava later. Turn the heat up to medium and let simmer until the liquid has thickened and reduced by a third (about 10 minutes—it will thicken more as it cools). Remove from the heat, stir in the rosewater, and set aside.

Remove the baklava from the oven and immediately pour the cooled syrup over the top. Let stand until fully absorbed. Serve with a strong, bitter Arabic coffee. Store in an airtight container, between layers of parchment (baking) paper.

Pistachio Baklava

PREPARATION TIME
35 minutes

COOKING TIME
45–50 minutes

MAKES
about 24 pieces

1 (9-oz/250-g) packet chilled (not frozen) phyllo (filo) pastry
1 ¾ sticks (7 oz/200 g) unsalted butter, melted

FOR THE FILLING
12 oz (350 g) raw, unsalted, shelled pistachio nuts, coarsely chopped
½ teaspoon ground ginger
seeds from 15 cardamom pods, coarsely ground in a pestle and mortar
½ teaspoon ground cinnamon
2 tablespoons sugar
2 tablespoons unsalted butter, melted
pinch of salt

FOR THE SYRUP
generous ½ cup (5 oz/150 g) honey
½ cup (3 ½ oz/100 g) superfine (caster) sugar
zest and juice of 1 lemon

See pages 240–241 for image

Another favorite to have with coffee are these spiced pistachio pastries. A lovely combination of aromatic spices and crisp layered pastry.

PREPARATION
First, make the filling. Put the pistachios into a large bowl with the ground ginger, ground cardamom seeds, cinnamon, sugar, melted butter, and salt, and mix well.

Unroll the chilled phyllo (filo) pastry sheets and cover with a damp cloth to prevent the sheets from drying out.

Preheat the oven to 325°F/160°C/Gas Mark 3.

Grease the bottom of a 8 x 12-inch (20 x 30-cm) roasting pan, then lay one of the shorter edges of the pastry along the long side of the roasting pan. Brush the pastry sheet with melted butter, then fold the sheet over on itself and brush the other side with butter as well. Repeat until you have 7 sheets of pastry, generously brushed with butter each time. Evenly scatter over a third of the filling, then cover with 6 sheets of buttered pastry. Scatter over another third of the filling, then cover with 4 sheets of buttered pastry, followed by the last third of the filling. Cover with the remaining pastry sheets and generously brush the final layer with butter.

Use a sharp knife to cut the baklava into 1 ¼-inch (3-cm) diamonds or squares. Carefully brush the remaining melted butter around evenly, focusing particularly on the cut edges. Bake in the center of the oven for 45–50 minutes or until golden, covering with aluminum foil after 30 minutes if the pastry is browning too quickly.

Meanwhile, make the syrup. Put the honey, sugar, and lemon juice into a small saucepan along with scant ½ cup (3 ½ fl oz/100 ml) of water. Gently warm in a small saucepan over low heat until the sugar has dissolved. Brush down the sides a few times with a wet pastry brush to get rid of any sugar crystals, as this may result in crystals forming in the baklava later. Let simmer until the liquid has thickened and reduced by a third (about 10 minutes). Remove from the heat and stir in the lemon zest and juice.

Remove the baklava from the oven and immediately pour the syrup over the top. Let cool completely, before lifting out the pieces of baklava. Serve with a strong, bitter Arabic coffee. Store in an airtight container, between layers of parchment (baking) paper.

1. Walnut and Rose Baklava (p.238) 2. Pecan and Orange Baklava (p.242) 3. Rose and Cardamom Shortbread (p.243) 4. Pistachio Baklava (p.239)

Pecan and Orange Baklava

PREPARATION TIME
35 minutes

COOKING TIME
45 minutes

MAKES
24 pieces

1 (9-oz/250-g) packet chilled (not frozen) phyllo (filo) pastry
1 ¾ sticks (7 oz/200 g) unsalted butter, melted

FOR THE FILLING
2 cups (9 oz/250 g) pecans (or a pecan and walnut mix)
1 cup (3 ½ oz/100 g) almond meal (ground almonds)
½ teaspoon ground cinnamon
½ teaspoon ground ginger
zest of 1 orange
2 tablespoons golden superfine (caster) sugar
pinch of fine sea salt
3 tablespoons unsalted butter, melted

FOR THE SYRUP
generous ½ cup (5 oz/150 g) honey
½ cup (3 ½ oz/100 g) caster sugar
juice of 1 lemon
1 tablespoon orange blossom water

See pages 240–241 for image

I like to make these around Christmas time – the orange zest and spices go so beautifully with the pecans.

PREPARATION
First, make the filling. Process the pecans in a food processor to coarse crumbs, then transfer to a mixing bowl and mix in the almond meal (ground almonds), spices, orange zest, sugar, sea salt, and melted butter. Stir until everything is evenly incorporated.

Unroll the chilled phyllo (filo) pastry sheets and cover with a damp cloth to prevent the sheets from drying out.

Preheat the oven to 325°F/160°C/Gas Mark 3.

Grease the bottom of a 8 x 12-inch (20 x 30-cm) roasting pan. Cut the pastry sheets to size to fit in the baking pan (don't worry if they tear and break—you'll have lots of layers to cover up any inconsistencies). Lay one of the sheets of pastry in the pan and brush with melted butter. Repeat until you have 8 sheets of pastry, generously brushed with butter each time. Evenly scatter over a third of the filling, then cover with 4 sheets of buttered pastry. Scatter over another third of the filling, then cover with 4 sheets of buttered pastry, followed by the last third of the filling. Cover with the remaining pastry sheets and generously brush the final layer with butter.

Use a sharp knife to cut the baklava into 1 ¼-inch (3-cm) diamonds or squares. Carefully brush the remaining melted butter around evenly, focusing particularly on the cut edges. Bake in the center of the oven for 45–50 minutes or until golden, covering with aluminum foil after 30 minutes if the pastry is browning too quickly.

Meanwhile, make the syrup. Put the honey, sugar, and lemon juice into a small saucepan along with scant ½ cup (3 ½ fl oz/100 ml) water and warm over medium-low heat until the sugar has dissolved, then increase the heat and boil to a syrupy consistency. Remove from the heat and let cool for 10 minutes, then stir in the orange blossom water.

Remove the baklava from the oven and immediately pour the syrup over the top. Let cool completely, before lifting out the pieces of baklava. Serve with a strong, bitter Arabic coffee. Store in an airtight container, between layers of parchment (baking) paper.

Rose and Cardamom Shortbread

PREPARATION TIME
15 minutes

COOKING TIME
55 minutes

MAKES
12–24 pieces, depending on size

1 ¾ sticks (7 oz/200 g) unsalted butter, softened, plus extra for greasing
½ cup (3 ½ oz/100 g) golden superfine (caster) sugar
2 teaspoons rosewater
1 cup (3 ½ oz/100 g) cornstarch (cornflour)
1 ½ cups (7 oz/200 g) all-purpose (plain) flour
seeds from 12 cardamom pods, coarsely bashed in a pestle and mortar
1 teaspoon sea salt
2 tablespoons rose sugar or 2 tablespoons of golden superfine (caster) sugar

See pages 240–241 for image

Rose sugar is available to buy in Middle Eastern stores or online. Fresh rose petals make for a pretty decoration too.

PREPARATION
Preheat the oven to 300°F/150°C/Gas Mark 2.

In a large bowl, beat the butter and sugar together with an electric handheld whisk until light and fluffy. Stir in the rosewater, then fold in the cornstarch (cornflour), all-purpose (plain) flour, cardamom seeds, and sea salt. Mix again with the whisk on a slow speed; the mixture will look like coarse crumbs but should come together when you pinch it between your fingers.

Generously grease a 8 x 12-inch (20 x 30-cm) baking pan, or 9-inch (22-cm) round cake pan, with butter. Press the shortbread mixture into the pan, pressing it down with the back of a wooden spoon so that it's well compacted and level, then pierce all over with a fork.

Bake for 55 minutes, until pale golden and firm to the touch.

Remove from the oven and use a sharp knife to immediately slice the shortbread into fingers, squares, or wedges. Scatter with the sugar of your choice and let cool completely, before lifting the shortbread pieces out of the pan with a blunt knife.

Stewed Plums with Orange

PREPARATION TIME
5 minutes

COOKING TIME
1 hour

SERVES
6–8

2 ¼ lb/1 kg plums, halved and pitted
⅓ cup (3 ½ oz/100 g) date molasses
2 orange slices
½ teaspoon ground cloves
½ teaspoon ground cinnamon

I like to have a big bowl of stewed fruit on standby in my house, and these plums always hit the spot. They make a great breakfast or pudding with a generous dollop of yogurt or ice cream!

PREPARATION
Put the plum halves into a large saucepan with the other ingredients and cover with generous 2 cups (17 fl oz/500 ml) water. Cook over low heat for 1 hour, stirring occasionally, until the plums have broken down.

Serve warm with thick Greek yogurt and a swirl of honey, or at room temperature alongside some granola.

Blood Orange and Pistachio Turkish Delight

PREPARATION TIME
30 minutes + overnight cooling

COOKING TIME
1 hour 30 minutes–2 hours

MAKES
36

6 blood oranges
3 ½ cups (1 lb 8 ½ oz/700 g) superfine (caster) sugar
juice of ½ lemon
1 teaspoon cream of tartar
1 ¼ cups (4 oz/120 g) cornstarch (cornflour)
⅓ cup (1 ½ oz/40 g) shelled pistachios, coarsely chopped
vegetable oil, for greasing

FOR THE COATING
½ cup (2 oz/50 g) cornstarch (cornflour)
scant ½ cup (2 oz/50 g) confectioners' (icing) sugar

See pages 248–249 for image

The added crunch of pistachios in this recipe is an amazing contrast to the smooth texture and zingy orange flavor.

Some recipes use gelatin for a firmer texture but I wanted to keep mine vegan, so expect it to be a little softer than some store-bought varieties. A sugar thermometer will give you the best results here—make sure you clip it to the side of the pan so you get a reading of the mixture and not the temperature of the bottom of the pan as I have done more than once!

PREPARATION

Juice the blood oranges into a strainer (sieve) set over a large measuring cup (measuring jug) or bowl until you have scant 1 cup (7 fl oz/200 ml) of juice. Pour the juice into a large, deep saucepan and add the sugar, lemon juice, and ¾ cup (6 fl oz/175 ml) water. Stir with a wooden spoon, then clip a sugar thermometer onto the side of the pan and bring to the boil over medium heat. Boil until the temperature of the mixture reaches 245°F/118°C—this should take around 15 minutes. Remove from the heat.

Put the cream of tartar into another large saucepan with the cornstarch (cornflour) and generous 2 cups (17 fl oz/500 ml) water. Cook the mixture over medium heat, using an electric handheld whisk to beat gently but constantly, for 2 minutes or until it thickens and turns from bright white to translucent—it should look like a very thick glue. Pour a ladleful of the sugar syrup into the pan and beat gently with the electric whisk until fully combined. Continue to introduce the sugar syrup in small amounts until it is fully combined and there are no lumps. Use a spatula to scrape around the edges, then beat again.

Turn the heat down to the lowest heat and cook for 60–90 minutes, stirring every 5 minutes with a wooden spoon, until the mixture has darkened a little and holds its shape when stirred. Stir through the nuts.

Line a 6 x 6-inch (15 x 15-cm) baking pan with plastic wrap (clingfilm), then grease lightly with vegetable oil. Use a spatula to turn the mixture into the pan and even out the surface (it can help to dip the spatula in hot water). Work as quickly as you can, as once it begins to set it is hard to work with. Cover and leave somewhere cool to cool overnight.

The next day, use a greased pizza cutter to cut the Turkish Delight into bite-size cubes. Sift together the cornstarch and confectioners' sugar for the coating, then toss the pieces through, until each cube is well covered.

Store at room temperature in an airtight container between layers of parchment (baking) paper. Add the rest of the cornstarch and sugar mixture to the box.

Orange and Hazelnut Turkish Delight

PREPARATION TIME
30 minutes + overnight cooling

COOKING TIME
2 hours 30 minutes

MAKES
25

3 ½ cups (1 lb 8 ½ oz/700 g) superfine (caster) sugar
scant 1 cup (7 fl oz/200 ml) orange juice
juice of ½ lemon
1 teaspoon cream of tartar
1 ¼ cups (4 oz/120 g) cornstarch (cornflour)
generous ⅓ cup (2 oz/50 g) toasted, skinned hazelnuts, coarsely chopped
1 tablespoon orange blossom water
vegetable oil, for greasing

FOR THE COATING
½ cup (2 oz/50 g) cornstarch (cornflour)
scant ½ cup (2 oz/50 g) confectioners' (icing) sugar

See pages 248–249 for image

This is another favorite recipe; again, the crunchy hazelnuts complement the smooth texture beautifully. Most modern recipes use gelatin, but the texture from this traditional method is quite different, and much more pleasing in my opinion.

PREPARATION
Pour the sugar, orange juice, lemon juice, and ¾ cup (6 fl oz/175 ml) cold water into a large, deep saucepan. Stir with a wooden spoon, then clip a sugar thermometer onto the side of the pan and bring to the boil over medium heat. Boil until the temperature of the mixture reaches 245°F/118°C—this should take around 15 minutes. Remove from the heat.

Put the cream of tartar into another large saucepan with the cornstarch (cornflour) and generous 2 cups (17 fl oz/500 ml) water. Cook the mixture over medium heat, using an electric handheld whisk to beat gently but constantly, for about 2 minutes or until it thickens and turns from bright white to translucent—it should look like a very thick glue. Pour a ladleful of the sugar syrup into the pan and beat gently with the electric whisk until fully combined. Continue to introduce the sugar syrup in small amounts until it is fully combined and there are no lumps. Use a spatula to scrape around the edges, then beat again.

Turn the heat down to the very lowest heat possible and cook for 90 minutes, stirring every 5 minutes with a wooden spoon, until the mixture has darkened a little and holds its shape when stirred. Stir through the hazelnuts and orange blossom water.

Line a 8 x 8-inch (20 x 20-cm) pan with plastic wrap (clingfilm), then grease lightly with vegetable oil. Use a spatula to turn the mixture into the pan and even out the surface (it can help to dip the spatula in hot water). Work as quickly as you can, as once it begins to set and is hard to work with. Cover and leave somewhere cool to cool overnight.

The next day, use a greased pizza cutter to cut the Turkish Delight into bite-size cubes. Sift together the cornstarch and confectioners' sugar for the coating, then toss the pieces through, until each cube is well covered.

Store at room temperature in an airtight container between layers of parchment (baking) paper. Add the rest of the cornstarch and sugar mixture to the box.

Blood Orange and Pistachio Turkish Delight (p.246) Orange and Hazelnut Turkish Delight (p.247)

CHAPTER NINE
Drinks

Beet Juice

PREPARATION TIME
15 minutes

COOKING TIME
—

SERVES
2

2 beets (beetroot), trimmed and peeled
½ orange, peeled
2 large carrots, peeled
2 apples, peeled and cored
apple juice, to dilute (optional)
plenty of ice, to serve

You can make so many combinations of delicious juices without the need for an expensive gadget. I like to put everything in my food processor or blender and then strain through a piece of cheesecloth (muslin), squeezing or pressing down firmly to get the last drops. Depending on how thick you like it, you can dilute it with a cloudy apple juice too.

PREPARATION
Blitz all the ingredients in a food processor or high-speed blender, then strain through cheesecloth (muslin), before serving over ice.

Orange Blossom Lemonade

PREPARATION TIME
10 minutes

COOKING TIME
—

SERVES
4

juice of 5 lemons
juice of 1 orange
½ cup (3 ½ oz/100 g) superfine (caster) sugar, or to taste
2 teaspoons orange blossom water, or to taste
generous 2 cups (18 fl oz/ 500 ml) sparkling or still water, chilled
plenty of ice, to serve
orange slices, to serve

A sparkling treat for sunny days. The orange blossom water really compliments the orange and lemon juice. As with rosewater, I find that different brands produce different strengths of orange blossom water, so I'll add a little at a time, tasting until I am happy with the end result.

PREPARATION
Add the juices, sugar, and orange blossom water to a large pitcher (jug), stirring well to combine and adjusting to taste. Top up with chilled water and serve over ice, garnished with orange slices.

Citrus and Pomegranate Wine

PREPARATION TIME
10 minutes

COOKING TIME
–

SERVES
6

1 (25-fl oz/750-ml) bottle fruity red wine
juice of 2 oranges
generous 2 cups (18 fl oz/ 500 ml) pomegranate juice
generous grating of nutmeg
5 cloves
plenty of ice, to serve

A sangria of sorts, this always goes down well with guests. To make it non-alcoholic, swap the wine for an apple juice that isn't too sweet. In the winter, I'll add a tablespoon or two of pomegranate molasses, and heat it before serving.

PREPARATION
Mix all the ingredients together, then strain to remove the cloves before serving over ice.

Iced Cardamom Coffee

PREPARATION TIME
10 minutes + 24 hours brewing

COOKING TIME
—

SERVES
4

seeds from 10 cardamom pods (pods discarded)
4 tablespoons freshly ground coffee
4 ¼ cups (34 fl oz/1 liter) filtered or bottled water
plenty of ice, to serve
almond milk, to serve (optional)

See pages 258–259 for image

This is an easy, at-home version of the very fashionable cold brew coffee, which I think has more of the delicacy of tea.

PREPARATION
Roughly bash the cardamom seeds in a pestle and mortar, then put into a pitcher (jug) with the coffee grounds. Slowly pour over the filtered water and stir to combine.

Cover and keep in a cool place for 24 hours, then strain through a coffee filter into another pitcher.

Serve over ice, with a splash of almond milk, if desired.

Rose and Cinnamon Tea

PREPARATION TIME
20 minutes

COOKING TIME
–

SERVES
4

2 tablespoons dried rose petals
zest of 1 orange (removed with a vegetable peeler)
1 cinnamon stick
few sprigs of mint
4 teaspoons honey, or to taste
1 tablespoon pomegranate seeds (optional)

See pages 258–259 for image

Here I use rose petals, together with fresh mint and cinnamon, to brew a refreshing tea.

PREPARATION
Measure out 3 cups (25 fl oz/750 ml) freshly boiled water into a pitcher (jug) and leave to cool for 1 minute. Add the rose petals, orange zest, cinnamon, and mint to a teapot, then pour over the hot water. Let steep for at least 15 minutes, then pour into glasses and stir in the honey to taste. Divide the pomegranate seeds among the glasses, if using.

1. Rose and Cinnamon Tea (p.257)

2. Hibiscus and Mint Iced Tea (p.260) 3. Warm Cardamom Milk (p.261) 4. Iced Cardamom Coffee (p.256) 5. Lebanese Cardamom Coffee (p.261)

Hibiscus and Mint Iced Tea

PREPARATION TIME
25 minutes + cooling time

COOKING TIME
5 minutes

SERVES
4

2 tablespoons hibiscus flowers
1 small bunch mint
scant ½ cup (3 ½ fl oz/100 ml) pomegranate juice
juice of 1 lemon,
plenty of ice, to serve
lemon slices, to serve

See pages 258–259 for image

The deep red flowers of the hibiscus plant make a delicious tea, with a taste not dissimilar to cranberry. I'll buy a big bag of dried flowers whenever I see them.

This iced tea reminds me of lazy lunches in the garden, with a few generations making up the party. The fruity flavor of hibiscus, as well as the fact that it's not bitter, make this an ideal drink to serve all ages.

PREPARATION
In a small saucepan, bring 2 ½ cups (20 fl oz/600 ml) water to the boil, then turn off the heat and add the hibiscus flowers and mint (reserving a few mint sprigs for garnish). Cover and let steep for 20 minutes.

Strain the tea into a pitcher (jug) and add the pomegranate and lemon juices. Chill in the refrigerator until ready to serve.

Serve over plenty of ice, garnished with lemon slices and fresh mint sprigs.

Warm Cardamom Milk

PREPARATION TIME	COOKING TIME	SERVES
25 minutes	5 minutes	2

1 ⅔ cups (14 fl oz/400 ml) milk of your choice
4 cardamom pods, smashed
1 ½ tablespoons honey, or to taste

See pages 258–259 for image

A soothing cupful, perfect just before bed.

PREPARATION
Combine the milk and cardamom in a small saucepan over a low heat. Gently heat until just warm, then remove from the heat and stir in the honey. Let steep for 20 minutes.

Strain, add honey to taste, and stir to combine. Gently warm again and serve.

Lebanese Cardamom Coffee

PREPARATION TIME	COOKING TIME	SERVES
5 minutes	about 15–20 minutes	4–6 (makes 1 rakwa or Lebanese coffee pot)

4 heaping tablespoons finely ground coffee
8 cardamom pods, lightly crushed in a pestle and mortar

See pages 258–259 for image

This is the only coffee my husband Heni will drink. In fact, lots of the coffee you buy in Lebanon has the cardamom already mixed in.

PREPARATION
Put the coffee into a stove-top coffee pot and pour in enough boiling water to fill it within 1 inch (2.5 cm) of the top. Bring to the boil, then remove from the heat and stir. Repeat 4–5 times, until the coffee no longer froths but boils smoothly. Add the cardamom pods and let steep over low heat for 5 minutes, then remove the pods with a spoon and serve.

Raspberry Rose Lemonade

PREPARATION TIME
10 minutes

COOKING TIME
—

SERVES
4

generous ¾ cup (5 oz/150 g) raspberries
juice of 4 lemons
2 generous tablespoons (1 oz/30 g) superfine (caster) sugar
2 teaspoons rosewater, or to taste
generous 2 cups (18 fl oz/ 500 ml) sparkling or still water, chilled
plenty of ice, to serve
lemon slices, to serve

Roses are prized in Lebanon. I learnt recently that British cuisine actually used them far more in years gone by, until vanilla became more widely available and took its place in puddings and desserts.

Rosewater can vary in strength and purity of flavor, depending on the brand you use. Start with less than you think you need, and add rosewater in small increments, according to your taste preference.

PREPARATION
Mash the raspberries in a bowl, then pass them through a strainer (sieve) set over a pitcher (jug), to remove the seeds. Add the lemon juice, sugar, and rosewater, stirring well to combine. Top up with chilled water and serve over plenty of ice, garnished with lemon slices.

Glossary

ALLSPICE
Known also as Jamaican pepper or pimenta, this spice is indispensable in the Middle East and is often used to season stews and meats. It is available whole or ground.

ALMONDS
A popular nut used to accent savory and sweet dishes. If a recipe calls for blanched almonds, simply soak whole nuts in boiled water for 15 minutes and drain. Press them between your fingers to remove the skins.

ARAK
This clear, colorless alcoholic drink from the Middle East has an anise flavor and makes a refreshing aperitif when combined with water and ice.

BAKLAVA
A sweet and rich pastry comprising layers of phyllo (filo) pastry, honey, and nuts.

BLACK PEPPER
Warm and intense, black peppercorns taste best when freshly ground, but pre-ground is fine for cooking.

BUCKWHEAT
Rich in soluble fiber, buckwheat is an excellent source of magnesium and calcium and contains eight essential amino acids.

BULGUR WHEAT
Bulgur is a form of cracked whole wheat that has been cleaned, parboiled, dried, and ground into particles to make it easy and quick to cook.

CARAWAY
Caraway, also known as meridian fennel, comes from the fruit of a plant that's related to parsley. Warm and slightly peppery, it has a distinctive taste and works best in the very traditional Lebanese rice pudding called Meghli.

CARDAMOM
Native to the Middle East, Africa, and Scandinavia, cardamom has a compelling spicy-sweet flavor that is unlike any other spice. Although cardamoms are available as pods or ground, it's best to buy them as whole pods so the seeds can be used when needed.

CAYENNE PEPPER
Intensely fiery and pungent, cayenne peppers are long, slender, and a vibrant red when mature. Dried and ground to a powder, cayenne is popular for adding heat to a dish.

CHICKPEAS
A widely used staple in the Lebanese diet, chickpeas are used in many traditional dishes, such as Classic Hummus (page 45) and Classic Falafel (page 44). Dried and canned chickpeas can be found in most supermarkets.

CHICKPEA FLOUR
Chickpea flour—also known as gram or besan flour—is naturally gluten-free and is a popular ingredient in both Middle Eastern and Indian cuisine.

CHILI (RED PEPPER) FLAKES/POWDER
A form of dried chile peppers, crushed or ground, that can be added in various amounts to soups or stews for extra heat.

CINNAMON
An aromatic and intrinsically sweet spice, cinnamon is popular in sweet pastries and desserts and adds an extra depth to savory stews.

CILANTRO (CORIANDER)
When using fresh leaves—known as cilantro—try stirring them into a dish just before serving. The ground seeds are used as a spice.

COUSCOUS (*SEE ALSO* MOGRABIEH)
Rolled semolina with a light and fluffy texture when steamed, couscous is commonly served with stews and makes a popular alternative to rice and pasta.

CUMIN
Available in seeds or ground, cumin has a strong and distinctive aroma and flavor.

DATES
At the heart of Middle Eastern cuisine and culture, there are hundreds of different species of dates, which can be enjoyed at various stages of ripeness. Completely ripe dates are most commonly eaten and their dense texture and sticky sweetness make them an excellent ingredient in cakes and sweet pastries.

FAVA (BROAD) BEANS
A staple in the Levant and Middle East, fava beans have been cultivated since ancient times. Best harvested when young and sweet, fava beans are used in soups, purees, salads, and stews, such as Ful Medames (page 175).

FENNEL SEEDS
Small, oblong, and ridged, fennel seeds come in a broad range of colors, from pale yellow-brown to green. They're highly aromatic and often confused with anise, which are similar in taste and appearance. Central and Eastern European cuisines use the seeds of wild, bitter fennel, which can be compared with celery seeds.

FENUGREEK
Fenugreek, or methi, is an aromatic herb that can be added to curries, dry rubs, and even bread recipes. It is available as fresh or dried leaves or as seeds. The latter are small, brownish yellow, and mildly bitter.

FETA CHEESE
Rich and creamy, feta is a soft and brined white curd cheese traditionally made with sheep milk, or with a combination of sheep and goat milk.

FREEKEH
A staple in the Middle East, freekeh is young green wheat that is roasted and cracked. It has a pleasant nutty flavor and texture.

GINGER
Fiery and aromatic fresh ginger can be used abundantly to add an extra base note to stews. Powdered dried ginger should be used more sparingly and lends itself more favorably to sweet baked goods and pastries.

GRAPE MOLASSES
Grape molasses is a thick, sweet syrup extracted from grapes. It is a natural sweetener and was traditionally used in Lebanese villages before refined white sugar was widely available. It also has a high content of iron and is used in treating iron-related anemia.

HALLOUMI
A semi-hard, unripened, brined cheese with a high melting point so it can be broiled (grilled). Springy, mild, and tangy, fried halloumi makes a quick and tasty appetizer or snack.

HONEY
Sticky, fragrant, and luxurious, honey makes an excellent natural sweetener and when baked, it gives a moist texture to cakes and pastries (but be careful when exposing it to heat, because it has a low burning point). It can also be drizzled over savory dishes, such as fried eggs, and used instead of sugar to sweeten your tea.

LABNEH
Labneh (page 10) is a type of Middle Eastern yogurt "cheese." It is made from strained youghurt, which gives it a thicker consistency and richness. When strained longer, it can be rolled into balls, flavored with herbs, and stored in oil.

LENTILS (GREEN/RED)
Lentils grow in pods and belong, with beans and peas, to the legume family. Low in fat and high in protein and fiber, they cook quickly, have a mild, earthy flavor, and are staples in the Middle Eastern pantry.

MAHLEB
Mahleb is an aromatic spice made from the ground pits of sour cherries. It is used in the Middle East to add a sweet-sour, nutty note to breads and cookies.

MOGRABIEH (*SEE ALSO* COUSCOUS)
Also known as Israeli, Lebanese, giant, or pearl couscous, mograbieh is a larger, slightly more doughy, version of the more familiar Moroccan couscous. Because of its size, it needs to be boiled instead of being steamed.

NUTMEG
A gentle and earthy spice, nutmeg goes especially well with greens, such as spinach. When possible, buy whole nutmeg and grate it yourself, because it has a much more vibrant flavor than store-bought ground powder.

OLIVE OIL
Drizzled over hot and cold mezze, the fruity, peppery flavor of olive oil is an essential part of Middle Eastern cuisine. The purer the oil, the lower the smoking point, so be sure to use regular (instead of extra-virgin) olive oil for frying.

ORANGE FLOWER WATER
Pungently aromatic, just a drop of this concentrated floral water adds an ever-so-slightly bitter citrus note to syrups, cakes, sweet pastries, and fresh lemonade.

PEANUTS
Nuts feature prominently in Middle Eastern dishes and peanuts, in particular, can be used in spice mixes, such as dukkah, or added for texture in stews and salads.

PHYLLO (FILO) PASTRY
The thin unleavened pastry dough used for making pastries such as baklava (pages 238–242).

PINE NUTS
Pine nuts are the edible kernels extracted from pine trees. Small and rich in flavor (especially when they're toasted), pine nuts are a staple in the Middle Eastern kitchen.

PISTACHIOS
Native to the Middle East, pistachios are a member of the cashew family and happen to be one of the most nutritious of all nuts. Finely chopped pistachios are often used as a pastry filling or dessert topping.

PITA
In the Middle East, flatbreads are served with almost every meal and one of the most popular is pita bread (page 200). Wonderfully versatile, the pita can be cut in half and act as a pocket for falafel or other hot food, or better yet, used to mop up sauces and stews.

POMEGRANATE
Native to Persia, the pomegranate is one of the oldest known fruits of the ancient world, and for centuries it has been revered for its flavor, color, and health benefits. Pomegranates are versatile, because they are not just popular in desserts, but they also add color, vibrancy, and sweetness to savory dishes.

POMEGRANATE MOLASSES
The sweet-sourness of pomegranates is amplified in this intense, thick syrup made from concentrated pomegranate juice. Use sparingly to add both acidity and sweetness to soups, stews, and stir-fried dishes.

PUMPKIN SEEDS
Pumpkin seeds contain concentrated sources of vitamins, minerals, and amino acids. They can be roasted and eaten whole as a snack, such as in the Za'atar Toasted Seed Mix (page 56), or used in vegetable or sweet dishes.

PUY LENTILS
Puy lentils from France are small and dark green with blue veining. They have a unique peppery flavor, retain their shape during cooking, and require less cooking time than ordinary green lentils.

QUINOA
Often referred to as a grain, quinoa is actually a seed from a vegetable related to Swiss chard, spinach, and beets (beetroot). It is not a traditional Middle Eastern grain, but I like to use it for its nutritional value (it's high in fiber and protein). It has a soapy coating known as saponin, a naturally occurring toxin, so it should always be rinsed thoroughly before preparation.

RICE
Whether as a supportive side dish or a hearty one-dish meal, rice plays an important role in Middle Eastern cuisine. Rice dishes are usually made with basmati rice (I also like brown rice) and can include a range of ingredients—such as raisins, pine nuts, or meat—depending on the region.

ROSEWATER
An intensely fragrant and evocative distillation made from steeping rose petals in water. Use sparingly to add a delicious floral note to lemonade, icings, syrups, and sweets, such as Walnut and Rose Baklava (page 238).

SEMOLINA
Semolina is a coarse grind of high-protein durum wheat kernels. Though commonly used for making pasta, semolina can also be used for making delicious traditional Lebanese cakes.

SESAME SEEDS
Touted as the "peanut" of the Middle East, sesame seeds are delicate and nutty in flavor. They are also used to make tahini, an essential Middle Eastern ingredient.

7-SPICE SEASONING
Lebanese 7-Spice Seasoning (page 12) or *baharat*—not to be confused with Arabic 7-spice—is a mixture of nutmeg, ginger, allspice, fenugreek, cloves, cinnamon, and black pepper. Store in an airtight glass jar.

SUMAC
Dark red sumac berries are usually available as a ground powder. They add a distinctive sour, citrus flavor to dishes and can be partnered with wild thyme and sesame seeds to make the spice blend Za'atar (see below and page 13).

TAHINI
Tahini (page 12) is a paste made from toasted, ground, hulled sesame seeds and is the basis for Middle Eastern dishes, such as hummus and halva. It's a staple of both Middle Eastern and Mediterranean cooking.

TURMERIC
Warm and earthy, with bitter undertones, this vibrant yellow spice is one of the key ingredients in Middle Eastern dishes. Traditionally, turmeric is used to add flavor and color to meat and vegetables in stews.

VEGETABLE BROTH (STOCK)
While it is not Middle Eastern tradition to add broth (stock) to grain dishes, I've incorporated it at times to help establish a depth of flavor in some of the recipes.

WALNUTS
In ancient Persia, walnuts were eaten only by royalty. They are a popular ingredient in sweet and savory Middle Eastern dishes and also form the basis for Muhammara (page 40), a tasty Lebanese dip.

ZA'ATAR
Za'atar is a variety of wild thyme that grows abundantly in the Middle East. It is also the name of a spice blend made from the wild thyme, ground sumac, and sesame seeds (see page 13). It can be used in meat and vegetable dishes.

Recipe Notes

Butter should always be unsalted.

Unless otherwise stated, all herbs are fresh and parsley is flat-leaf parsley.

Pepper is always freshly ground black pepper, unless otherwise specified.

Eggs, vegetables, and fruits are assumed to be large (UK: medium) size, unless otherwise specified.

Milk is always full-fat (whole), unless otherwise specified.

Garlic cloves are assumed to be large; use two if small.

Cooking and preparation times are for guidance only, as individual ovens vary. If using a fan (convection) oven, follow the manufacturer's instructions concerning oven temperatures.

Some of the recipes require advanced techniques, specialist equipment, and professional experience to achieve good results.

To test whether your deep-frying oil is hot enough, add a cube of stale bread. If it browns in thirty seconds, the temperature is 350–375°F (180–190°C), about right for most frying. Exercise a high level of caution when following recipes involving any potentially hazardous activity, including the use of high temperature and open flames. In particular, when deep-frying, add the food carefully to avoid splashing, wear long sleeves, and never leave the pan unattended.

Some recipes include raw or very lightly cooked eggs. These should be avoided particularly by the elderly, infants, pregnant women, convalescents, and anyone with an impaired immune system.

Both metric and imperial measures are used in this book. Follow one set of measurements throughout, not a mixture, as they are not interchangeable.

All spoon measurements are level.
1 teaspoon = 5 ml; 1 tablespoon = 15 ml. Australian standard tablespoons are 20 ml, so Australian readers are advised to use 3 teaspoons in place of 1 tablespoon when measuring small quantities.

When no quantity is specified, for example of oils, salts, and herbs used for finishing dishes, quantities are discretionary and flexible.

Index

Page numbers in **bold** refer to illustrations

A
aioli, za'atar 48, **50**
almond milk: baked cardamom and almond milk rice pudding 228, **229**
anchovies, mini flatbreads with lamb and 61, **62**
apples
    cabbage and apple slaw **79**, 117
    pickled apple 66, **67**
    tahini rémoulade 78, **79**
apricots
    apricots with mascarpone 232, **233**
    large chicken kibbeh with apricots 182, **183**
Arabic coffee mousse 234, **235**
artichokes
    crispy artichoke hearts with za'atar aioli 48, **50**
    fava bean and artichoke tartlets **205**, 206
    lemon artichoke dip **35**, 36

B
babaganoush 32, **35**
baklava 264
    pecan and orange baklava **241**, 242
    pistachio baklava 239, **240**
    walnut and rose baklava 238, **240**
batata harra, classic 106, **109**
beets (beetroot)
    beet and chickpea fritters 130, **133**
    beet and chocolate mousse cakes 220, **221**
    beet juice 252, **253**
    pink pickled turnips **14**, 16
    rainbow beet salad with walnut pesto **72**, 74
    roasted baby beets with za'atar labneh 38, **39**
    scrambled egg with salmon and beets 142, **143**
    toasted quinoa with beets, olives, and orange 160, **161**
bread
    bulgur wheat bread with za'atar 196, **197**
    favorite manoushe with new toppings 188–9, **190–1**
    fish shawarma 216, **217**
    halloumi-stuffed loaf 198, **199**
    mini flatbreads with crab and salmon 60, **63**
    mini flatbreads with lamb and anchovies 61, **62**
    pita bread 200, **201**
    scrambled egg with salmon and beets 142, **143**
    sweet blessed buns 194, **195**
brownies, tahini 223, **224**
Brussels sprouts: shredded Brussels sprouts with walnuts 92, **93**
buckwheat: za'atar mushrooms with buckwheat pancakes 94, **95**
bulgur wheat 264
    bulgur wheat bread with za'atar 196, **197**
    golden bulgur wheat with crushed roasted carrots 154, **155**
    large chicken kibbeh with apricots 182, **183**
    large lamb kibbeh 184, **185**
    lentil and bulgur wheat m'juderah 178, **179**
    little Damascus kibbeh with pine nuts 46, **47**
    winter tabbouleh 70, **73**
buns, sweet blessed 194, **195**
butter, lemon parsley **191**, 192
butternut squash
    butternut squash, cavolo nero, and freekeh 156, **157**
    roasted squash with Middle Eastern spices 114, **115**
    whole baked squash with quinoa 170, **173**

C
cabbage
    cabbage and apple slaw **79**, 117
    red cabbage and pomegranate **119**, 121
cakes
    pistachio and pomegranate cake **224**, 227
    tahini brownies 223, **224**
cardamom 264
    Arabic coffee mousse 234, **235**
    baked cardamom and almond milk rice pudding 228, **229**
    iced cardamom coffee 256, **258**
    Lebanese cardamom coffee **258**, 261
    rose and cardamom shortbread **241**, 243
    sweet blessed buns 194, **195**
    warm cardamom milk 259
carrots
    carrot and pistachio fritters 131, **132**
    citrus-glazed carrots with spiced pistachios 84, **85**
    golden bulgur wheat with crushed roasted carrots 154, **155**
    spiced pickled carrots **15**, 17
cauliflower
    cauliflower couscous with pine nuts and raisins 82, **83**
    charred cauliflower with pickled apple 66, **67**
    potato, cauliflower, and turmeric fritters **132**, 135
    roasted cauliflower with tahini and smoky paprika 88, **89**
    turmeric-pickled cauliflower 18, **19**
cavolo nero: butternut squash, cavolo nero, and freekeh 156, **157**
celery root (celeriac)
    celery root with toasted spices 104, **105**
    tahini rémoulade 78, **79**
chicken
    chicken fatteh 212, **213**
    large chicken kibbeh with apricots 182, **183**
chicken livers with garlic and lemon sauce 140, **141**
chickpea (gram/besan) flour 264
    chickpea and za'atar crackers 203, **204**
chickpeas 264
    beet and chickpea fritters 130, **133**
    chickpea savory pancake with za'atar **190**, 193
    classic falafels **43**, 44
    classic hummus **43**, 45
    creamed chickpeas 66, **67**
    griddled lettuce salad with crispy chickpeas **73**, 75
    hummus with lamb and pine nuts 58, **59**
    spiced chickpea popcorn 41, **42**
chilies 264
    kale and chile rolls 208, **209**
    tomato and chili relish 54, **55**
chips, toasted pita 54, **55**
chocolate
    Arabic coffee mousse 234, **235**
    beet and chocolate mousse cakes 220, **221**
    tahini brownies 223, **224**
citrus fruit
    citrus and pomegranate wine 254, **255**
    citrus-glazed carrots with spiced pistachios 84, **85**
    citrus yogurt sauce 168, **169**
clementine salad with black olives 76, **77**
coffee
    Arabic coffee mousse 234, **235**
    iced cardamom coffee 256, **258**
    Lebanese cardamom coffee **258**, 261
cookies
    favorite ma'mool cookies 222, **225**
    rose and cardamom shortbread **241**, 243
couscous
    mograbieh salad 71, **73**
    seeded couscous tabbouleh **173**, 174
crabmeat: mini flatbreads with crab and salmon 60, **63**
crackers
    chickpea and za'atar crackers 203, **204**
    cumin seed crackers 202, **204**
curry: fried sea bass with tahini and curry sauce 146, **147**

D

Damascus kibbeh with pine nuts 46, **47**
dates 264
    favorite ma'mool cookies 222, **225**
dips
    babaganoush 32, **35**
    classic hummus **43**, 45
    garlic dip 148, **149**
    lemon artichoke dip **35**, 36
    muhammara 40, **43**
    tahini and grape molasses dip 33, **34**
dressings
    olive, lemon and dill dressing **23**, 25
    preserved lemon dressing 20, **23**
    smoky paprika dressing 88, **89**
    spicy tahini dressing **22**, 24
    yogurt and lemon zest dressing 21, **23**

E

eggplants (aubergines)
    babaganoush 32, **35**
    crispy eggplant with grape molasses 112, **113**
    eggplant rice rolls 162, **163**
    smoky eggplant and cilantro tartlets **205**, 207
    upside down eggplants 180, **181**
eggs
    beet and chickpea fritters 130, **133**
    carrot and pistachio fritters 131, **132**
    scrambled egg with salmon and beets 142, **143**
    shakshuka 96, **97**
    Turkish scrambled eggs 126, **127**
    zucchini and mint fritters **133**, 134
    zucchini kuku **118**, 120

F

falafels, classic **43**, 44
farina: little Damascus kibbeh with pine nuts 46, **47**
farro: baked farro with feta, herbs, and olives 171, **173**
fasolia 158, **159**
fatteh
    chicken fatteh 212, **213**
    saffron rice and vegetable fatteh 152, **153**
fava (broad beans) 264
    fasolia 158, **159**
    fava bean and artichoke tartlets **205**, 206
    ful medames **172**, 175
fennel
    fried potatoes with fennel and green olives **109**, 111
    stuffed peppers with quinoa 136, **137**
    winter tabbouleh 70, **73**
feta cheese 265
    baked farro with feta, herbs, and olives 171, **173**
    kale and chile rolls 208, **209**
    pickled peppers stuffed with feta **34**, 37

quick orzo with kale and sumac 176, **177**
stuffed peppers with quinoa 136, **137**
whole baked squash with quinoa 170, **173**
za'atar mushrooms with buckwheat pancakes 94, **95**
figs
    fig and rose jam 28, **29**
    labneh with figs and candied walnuts 80, **81**
fish
    cod goujons with garlic dip 148, **149**
    fish shawarma 216, **217**
    fried sea bass with tahini and curry sauce 146, **147**
    mini flatbreads with crab and salmon 60, **63**
    mini flatbreads with lamb and anchovies 61, **62**
    pan-fried sardines 144, **145**
    scrambled egg with salmon and beets 142, **143**
flatbreads
    fish shawarma 216, **217**
    mini flatbreads with crab and salmon 60, **63**
    mini flatbreads with lamb and anchovies 61, **62**
    scrambled egg with salmon and beets 142, **143**
freekeh 265
    butternut squash, cavolo nero, and freekeh 156, **157**
fritters
    beet and chickpea fritters 130, **133**
    carrot and pistachio fritters 131, **132**
    potato, cauliflower, and turmeric fritters **132**, 135
    zucchini and mint fritters **133**, 134
ful medames **172**, 175

G

garlic
    garlic and lemon sauce 140, **141**
    garlic dip 148, **149**
goujons, cod 148, **149**
grape molasses 265
    crispy eggplant with grape molasses 112, **113**
    tahini and grape molasses dip 33, **34**
green beans
    fasolia 158, **159**
    green bean and hazelnut salad 68, **69**

H

halloumi 265
    grilled purple sprouting broccoli and halloumi 116, **118**
    halloumi-stuffed loaf 198, **199**
    spiced red lentil koftas 168, **169**
harissa sweet potato cakes 128, **129**
hazelnuts

green bean and hazelnut salad 68, **69**
orange and hazelnut Turkish delight 247, **249**
hibiscus and mint iced tea **259**, 260
hummus
    classic hummus **43**, 45
    hummus with lamb and pine nuts 58, **59**

I

iced drinks
    hibiscus and mint iced tea **259**, 260
    iced cardamom coffee 256, **258**

J

jam, fig and rose 28, **29**
Jerusalem artichoke and orange soup 122, **123**
juice, beet 252, **253**

K

kale
    kale and chile rolls 208, **209**
    quick orzo with kale and sumac 176, **177**
kibbeh
    large chicken kibbeh with apricots 182, **183**
    large lamb kibbeh 184, **185**
    little Damascus kibbeh with pine nuts 46, **47**
koftas, spiced red lentil 168, **169**
kuku, zucchini **118**, 120

L

labneh 10, **11**, 265
    labneh with figs and candied walnuts 80, **81**
    orange blossom labneh with honey and pistachios 189, **191**
    orange blossom labneh with squash 98, **99**
    roasted baby beets with za'atar labneh 38, **39**
lamb
    homemade spicy lamb sausage 138, **139**
    hummus with lamb and pine nuts 58, **59**
    lamb manakish 214, **215**
    large lamb kibbeh 184, **185**
    mini flatbreads with lamb and anchovies 61, **62**
    upside down eggplants 180, **181**
Lebanese cardamom coffee **258**, 261
Lebanese 7-spice seasoning 12, **15**, 266
    fried potatoes with 107, **108**
lemonade
    orange blossom lemonade 252, **253**
    raspberry rose lemonade 262, **263**
lemons
    fried potatoes with preserved lemon and mint **109**, 110

garlic and lemon sauce 140, **141**
lemon artichoke dip **35**, 36
lemon parsley butter **191**, 192
lemon tahini sauce 162, **163**
olive, lemon and dill dressing **23**, 25
orange blossom lemonade 252, **253**
preserved lemon and bay-scented olives 49, **51**
preserved lemon dressing 20, **23**
preserved lemons with bay and cinnamon 26, **27**
raspberry rose lemonade 262, **263**
yogurt and lemon zest dressing 21, **23**
lentils 265
    lentil and bulgur wheat m'juderah 178, **179**
    lentils with slow-roasted tomatoes and thyme 166, **167**
    spiced red lentil koftas 168, **169**
lettuce
    fish shawarma 216, **217**
    griddled lettuce salad with crispy chickpeas **73**, 75

M

ma'mool cookies, favorite 222, **225**
manakish, lamb 214, **215**
manoushe: favorite manoushe with new toppings 188–9, **190–1**
mascarpone, apricots with 232, **233**
milk, warm cardamom **259**, 261
m'juderah, lentil and bulgur wheat 178, **179**
mograbieh (giant couscous) 265
    mograbieh salad 71, **73**
mousse, Arabic coffee 234, **235**
mousse cakes, beet and chocolate 220, **221**
muhammara 40, **43**
mushrooms: za'atar mushrooms with buckwheat pancakes 94, **95**

O

olives
    baked farro with feta, herbs, and olives 171, **173**
    clementine salad with black olives 76, **77**
    fried potatoes with fennel and green olives **109**, 111
    olive, lemon and dill dressing **23**, 25
    orange, rosemary, and coriander olives **51**, 52
    preserved lemon and bay-scented olives 49, **51**
    seeded pomegranate olives **51**, 53
    toasted quinoa with beets, olives, and orange 160, **161**
onions roasted with orange and thyme 90, **91**
orange blossom water 265
    orange blossom labneh with honey and pistachios 189, **191**
orange blossom labneh with squash 98, **99**
orange blossom lemonade 252, **253**
orange blossom water saffron tartlets **224**, 226
oranges
    blood orange and pistachio Turkish delight 246, **248**
    blood orange and pomegranate sorbet 230, **231**
    Jerusalem artichoke and orange soup 122, **123**
    onions roasted with orange and thyme 90, **91**
    orange and hazelnut Turkish delight 247, **249**
    orange blossom lemonade 252, **253**
    orange, rosemary, and coriander olives **51**, 52
    pecan and orange baklava **241**, 242
    stewed plums with orange 244, **245**
    toasted quinoa with beets, olives, and orange 160, **161**

P

pancakes
    buckwheat pancakes 94, **95**
    chickpea savory pancake with za'atar **190**, 193
pasta: quick orzo with kale and sumac 176, **177**
pecan and orange baklava **241**, 242
peppers
    muhammara 40, **43**
    pickled peppers stuffed with feta **34**, 37
    stuffed peppers with quinoa 136, **137**
pesto, walnut **72**, 74
phyllo (filo) pastry 265
    kale and chile rolls 208, **209**
    pecan and orange baklava **241**, 242
    pistachio baklava 239, **240**
    spinach and walnut tartlets 210, **211**
    walnut and rose baklava 238, **240**
pickles
    pickled apples 66, **67**
    pickled peppers stuffed with feta **34**, 37
    pink pickled turnips 14, **16**
    spiced pickled carrots **15**, 17
    turmeric-pickled cauliflower 18, **19**
pine nuts 266
    cauliflower couscous with pine nuts and raisins 82, **83**
    hummus with lamb and pine nuts 58, **59**
    little Damascus kibbeh with pine nuts 46, **47**
pistachios 26
    blood orange and pistachio Turkish delight 246, **248**
    carrot and pistachio fritters 131, **132**
    citrus-glazed carrots with spiced pistachios 84, **85**
    favorite ma'mool cookies 222, **225**
    orange-blossom labneh with honey and pistachios 189, **191**
    pistachio and pomegranate cake **224**, 227
    pistachio baklava 239, **240**
pita breads 200, **201**, 266
    chicken fatteh 212, **213**
    toasted pita chips 54, **55**
plums: stewed plums with orange 244, **245**
pomegranate syrup: red cabbage and pomegranate **119**, 121
pomegranates 266
    blood orange and pomegranate sorbet 230, **231**
    citrus and pomegranate wine 254, **255**
    pistachio and pomegranate cake **224**, 227
potatoes
    classic batata harra 106, **109**
    fried potatoes with fennel and green olives **109**, 111
    fried potatoes with Lebanese 7-spice sauce 107, **108**
    fried potatoes with preserved lemon and mint **109**, 110
    little Damascus kibbeh with pine nuts 46, **47**
    potato, cauliflower, and turmeric fritters **132**, 135
pul biber
    stuffed peppers with quinoa 136, **137**
    sweet potatoes with tahini and pul biber 102, **103**
purple sprouting broccoli and halloumi, grilled 116, **118**

Q

quinces poached in their own syrup 236, **237**
quinoa 266
    stuffed peppers with quinoa 136, **137**
    toasted quinoa with beets, olives, and orange 160, **161**
    whole baked squash with quinoa 170, **173**

R

raisins, cauliflower couscous with pine nuts and 82, **83**
raspberry rose lemonade 262, **263**
relish, tomato and chili 54, **55**
rémoulade, tahini 78, **79**
rice 266
    baked cardamom and almond milk rice pudding 228, **229**
    eggplant rice rolls 162, **163**
    saffron rice and vegetable fatteh 152, **153**
    upside down eggplants 180, **181**

wild rice salad with roasted root vegetables 164, **165**
rose petals: rose and cinnamon tea 257, **258**
rosewater 266
   fig and rose jam 28, **29**
   raspberry rose lemonade 262, **263**
   rose and cardamom shortbread **241**, 243
   walnut and rose baklava 238, **240**

S
saffron
   orange blossom water saffron tartlets **224**, 226
   saffron rice and vegetable fatteh 152, **153**
salads 64–85
   cabbage and apple slaw **79**, 117
   clementine salad with black olives 76, **77**
   green bean and hazelnut salad 68, **69**
   griddled lettuce salad with crispy chickpeas **73**, 75
   mograbieh salad 71, **73**
   rainbow beet salad with walnut pesto **72**, 74
   seeded couscous tabbouleh **173**, 174
   wild rice salad with roasted root vegetables 164, **165**
   winter tabbouleh 70, **73**
sausages
   homemade spicy lamb sausage 138, **139**
   lamb manakish 214, **215**
seasonings, Lebanese 7-spice 12, **15**
seeds
   seeded couscous tabbouleh **173**, 174
   za'atar toasted seed mix 56, **57**
sesame seeds
   tahini 12, **15**
   za'atar 13, **14**
shakshuka 96, **97**
shawarma, fish 216, **217**
shortbread, rose and cardamom **241**, 243
sorbet, blood orange and pomegranate 230, **231**
soup, Jerusalem artichoke and orange 122, **123**
spices
   celery root with toasted spices 104, **105**
   Lebanese 7-spice seasoning 12, **15**, 107, **108**, 266
   roasted squash with Middle Eastern spices 114, **115**
spinach and walnut tartlets 210, **211**
squash
   butternut squash, cavolo nero, and freekeh 156, **157**
   orange blossom labneh with squash 98, **99**
   roasted squash with Middle Eastern spices 114, **115**
   whole baked squash with quinoa 170, **173**
stews: fasolia 158, **159**
sumac 266
   quick orzo with kale and sumac 176, **177**
   roasted turnips with sumac and fresh thyme 100, **101**
sweet blessed buns 194, **195**
sweet potatoes
   harissa sweet potato cakes 128, **129**
   sweet potatoes with tahini and pul biber 102, **103**
Swiss chard: manoushe with Swiss chard and nutmeg 189, **190**

T
tabbouleh
   seeded couscous tabbouleh **173**, 174
   winter tabbouleh 70, **73**
tahini 12, **15**, 266
   babaganoush 32, **35**
   classic hummus **43**, 45
   fried sea bass with tahini and curry sauce 146, **147**
   hummus with lamb and pine nuts 58, **59**
   lemon tahini sauce 162, **163**
   roasted cauliflower with tahini and smoky paprika 88, **89**
   spicy tahini dressing **22**, 24
   sweet potatoes with tahini and pul biber 102, **103**
   tahini and grape molasses dip 33, **34**
   tahini brownies 223, **224**
   tahini rémoulade 78, **79**
tartlets
   fava bean and artichoke tartlets **205**, 206
   orange blossom water saffron tartlets **224**, 226
   smoky eggplant and cilantro tartlets **205**, 207
   spinach and walnut tartlets 210, **211**
tea
   hibiscus and mint iced tea **259**, 260
   rose and cinnamon 257, **258**
tomatoes
   fried potatoes with Lebanese 7-spice sauce 107, **108**
   lentils with slow-roasted tomatoes and thyme 166, **167**
   shakshuka 96, **97**
   tomato and chili relish with toasted pita chips 54, **55**
Turkish delight
   blood orange and pistachio Turkish delight 246, **248**
   orange and hazelnut Turkish delight 247, **249**
Turkish scrambled eggs 126, **127**
turmeric
   potato, cauliflower, and turmeric fritters **132**, 135
   turmeric-pickled cauliflower 18, **19**
turnips
   pink pickled turnips 14, **16**
   roasted turnips with sumac and fresh thyme 100, **101**

U
upside down eggplants 180, **181**

V
vegetables 86–123
   saffron rice and vegetable fatteh 152, **153**
   wild rice salad with roasted root vegetables 164, **165**
   see also squash; turnips, *etc*

W
walnuts 267
   favorite ma'mool cookies 222, **225**
   labneh with figs and candied walnuts 80, **81**
   muhammara 40, **43**
   shredded Brussels sprouts with walnuts 92, **93**
   spinach and walnut tartlets 210, **211**
   walnut and rose baklava 238, **240**
   walnut pesto **72**, 74
wine, citrus and pomegranate 254, **255**
winter tabbouleh 70, **73**

Y
yogurt
   citrus yogurt sauce 168, **169**
   garlic dip 148, **149**
   labneh 10, **11**
   orange blossom labneh with squash 98, **99**
   yogurt and lemon zest dressing 21, **23**
   yogurt sauce 212, **213**

Z
za'atar 13, **14**, 267
   bulgur wheat bread with za'atar 196, **197**
   chickpea and za'atar crackers 203, **204**
   chickpea savory pancake with za'atar **190**, 193
   roasted baby beets with za'atar labneh 38, **39**
   za'atar aioli 48, **50**
   za'atar mushrooms with buckwheat pancakes 94, **95**
   za'atar toasted seed mix 56, **57**
zucchini (courgettes)
   zucchini and mint fritters **133**, 134
   zucchini kuku **118**, 120

Dedication

I dedicate this book to my son Joe and grandson George, without whom none of this would be possible. I'd also like to extend a special heartfelt thanks to Jess, Anna, and Lucie for their contributions and commitment. Tom and Anna continue to inspire me with the light they bring to my life. And lastly, I offer deep gratitude to Emilia, Ellie, Eve, Liz, Max, and all of our talented and dedicated testers for their involvement in the book. I will be eternally grateful to you all.

Phaidon Press Limited
Regent's Wharf
All Saints Street
London N1 9PA

Phaidon Press Inc.
65 Bleecker Street
New York, NY 10012

phaidon.com

First published 2018
© 2018 Phaidon Press Limited

ISBN 978 0 7148 7685 6

A CIP catalogue record for this book is available from the British Library and the Library of Congress.

All rights reserved. No part of this publication may be reproduced, stored in a retrieval system or transmitted, in any form or by any means, electronic, mechanical, photocopying, recording or otherwise, without the written permission of Phaidon Press Limited.

Commissioning Editor: Eve O'Sullivan
Project Editor: Ellie Smith
Production Controller: Lisa Fiske
Design: Aaron Garza
Photography: Liz and Max Haarala Hamilton

Printed in China

The publisher would like to thank Sophie Foot, Joe Hage, Taahir Husain, Katie Marshall, Pene Parker, Lisa Pendreigh, Emily Preece-Morrison, Anna Shepherd, Lucie Ware, and Holly Wulff-Petersen for their contributions to the book.